JN302880

MEG
the Miracle Idol
ミラクルアイドルメグ

Vol. 1

You can be a Star!
［アイドルなんて、なるしかない！］

安河内哲也
a.k.a.
Ted Eguchi

Illustration：**碧風羽**

多読のすすめ

楽しめば楽しむほど、英語は読めるようになる!

　「英文多読シリーズ」は、読み出すと止まらない、ワクワクストーリーで、英語を読むことを純粋に楽しむためのものです。皆さんは、これを読み始めると、きっとストーリーの世界にハマってしまうでしょう。

　授業や参考書で精読を学び、それを繰り返し復習するのも大切な勉強です。しかし、それだけでは英文に触れる量が絶対的に不足してしまいます。ただ机で「勉強」しているだけでは、言語の修得に必要な反射神経がなかなか身に付かないのです。

　そこで、たくさんの英語に触れ、慣れるための、「多読」が必要になります。「多読」の秘訣は、勉強ではなく純粋に読書として英文を楽しむことです。

　日本語の読解も、勉強して覚えたわけではありませんよね。マンガや小説など、大好きな本を読みながら覚えたはずです。この小説は、難しい単語や構文を極力使わずに、シンプルな英語で読みやすく書かれています。でも、本当に大切な単語や熟語、構文はしっかり文の中に組み込んであります。

　「多読」のためには……
①普段勉強しているレベルより簡単であること
②内容が楽しく、興味が持てるものであること
③辞書を引いて調べることによって、読書が中断されないようにすること

　この三つが大切です。また、従来の多読教材では、「内容は簡単だけれど、語彙や表現のレベルが高すぎて読書が止まってしまう。」「内容が日本人にとっていまいち興味が持てない。」という声がよく聞かれました。

そこで、このシリーズでは以下の工夫をしました。
◎語彙のレベルや文法のレベルを制約して、おおむね英検準2級〜センター基礎レベルの英語で、オリジナルストーリーとして書き起こした。
◎日本人、特に若者にとって興味が持てる内容を題材とした。イラストを随所にちりばめ読みやすくし、一度読み出すと止められなくなる工夫をした。
◎単語が気になる場合でも、すぐに解決できる語句注を充実させた。
◎朗読音声を無料でダウンロードできるようにし、耳からもストーリーが楽しめるようにした。(英語・日本語・日英対訳)
◎一冊分のストーリーの長さを5,000〜6,000語程度とし、ある程度読み応えはあるが、長過ぎて嫌にならないところでストーリーを完結させた。

http://www.toshin.com/books/
※音声ダウンロードの際は、下記のパスワードが必要です。
詳細は上記のサイトをご参照ください。
Password : **BHs5QfRW**
　　　　　　　　　　　エフ

　このような学習効果を、綿密に計算してこのシリーズは作成されています。とは言っても、何より多読では、勉強のことを忘れて、純粋に楽しむことが重要です。いつでも、どこでも読んで読んで読みまくることによって、知らず知らずのうちに試験の英文も読めるようになってしまう。そんな人がたくさん生まれることを願っています。

　英語だけで楽しむもよし、訳や単語・熟語の注釈を見ながら楽しむもよし、CDの朗読を聞いて楽しむのもよし。最後まで、約5,000語の冒険の旅へと出かけましょう。

安河内哲也 a.k.a. Ted Eguchi

Contents

Chapter 1	Where're Mom and Dad?	5
Chapter 2	The House is Gone.	15
Chapter 3	Easy Homeless Life	23
Chapter 4	Unhappy Birthday	31
Chapter 5	Is He a Hero or ...?	37
Chapter 6	Won't You be an Idol?	45
Chapter 7	The Transformation	55
Chapter 8	Can You Sing a Song?	63
Chapter 9	Akihabara	71
Chapter 10	Just Keep Smiling!	81
Chapter 11	Will You be my Daughter?	93
Chapter 12	The First Lesson	101
Chapter 13	I will be a Star, not You.	109
Chapter 14	I will Fly High for You.	117
和訳		123
索引		149

MEG
the Miracle Idol

Vol. 1

You can be a Star!

Chapter 1

Where're Mom and Dad?

MEG the Miracle Idol Vol.1
Where're Mom and Dad?

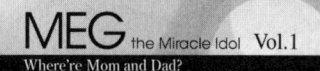

Where're Mom and Dad?

Meg Suzuki was born in an old suburb of Tokyo. Her father owned a small factory that produced small parts for cars. Her mother helped him there. It was a small factory with four workers, for whom Meg's father could barely pay weekly wages. They were always busy, and didn't talk much with Meg. They rarely had meals together with Meg.

When Meg was in elementary school, her friends

WORD LIST

☐ be born	熟生まれる	☐ weekly	形週に一度の
☐ suburb	名郊外	☐ wage	名賃金、給料
☐ own	動所有する	☐ talk with ～	熟～と話す
☐ factory	名工場	☐ rarely	副めったに ..... ない
☐ produce	動生産する	☐ together	副一緒に
☐ help	動手伝う、助ける	☐ when	接 ..... とき
☐ barely	副かろうじて、やっと	☐ elementary school	熟小学校
☐ pay	動支払う		

always talked about the theme parks and the movies they went to, but Meg couldn't join their conversations. Even on Sundays, her mother worked and had no time or money to take Meg anywhere. Her father was seldom at home on his days off. He usually went to horse races, pachinko parlors, or some other gambling places. Even when he was at home, he was drunk and yelled at her mother. He often beat Meg and her mother.

Unlike her friends, Meg didn't have pretty clothes,

WORD LIST			
☐ talk about ~	熟~について話す	☐ horse race	熟競馬
☐ theme park	熟テーマパーク	☐ pachinko parlor	熟パチンコ店
☐ join	動加わる	☐ gambling place	熟賭博場
☐ conversation	名会話	☐ drunk	形酔っ払って
☐ even ~	前~でさえ	☐ yell at ~	熟~を怒鳴りつける
☐ anywhere	副どこにも	☐ beat	動打つ、殴る、たたく
☐ seldom	副めったに.....ない	☐ unlike ~	前~と違って
☐ at home	熟在宅して	☐ clothes	名衣服
☐ day off	熟休日		

fancy toys or video games. She always wore a white T-shirt and tattered jeans. Her hair was messy, and she looked like a boy. She had cute, big eyes, but cheap silver-framed glasses with thick lenses hid them from the world.

In junior high school, the kids in her class began picking on her, so she began to cut classes and to stay home watching television. Television was her only friend. She saw a dreamy world through the television screen. It was the only escape from her miserable life.

Meg wished to live in that world beyond the television screen. Ever since she was very little, she had loved to imitate pop stars. Because she didn't have anything else to do, she loved singing and dancing. Now she could sing and dance pretty well, although she was not sure if she was any good herself.

Her hero was a very popular idol named Momo Sakura. She was very pretty, and she sang very well.

WORD LIST

☐ miserable	形惨めな、不幸な
☐ life	名生活、生命、人生
☐ wish to V	熟 V したいと思う（願う）
☐ beyond ~	前～の向こうの
☐ ever since	熟 ..... 以来ずっと（今まで）
☐ imitate	動まねる、見習う
☐ pop star	熟人気歌手
☐ because	接 ..... なので
☐ else	副その他に
☐ pretty well	熟かなりよく
☐ although	接しかし
☐ be not sure if S V	熟 S が V するかどうかわからない
☐ oneself	代自分自身
☐ hero	名英雄
☐ popular idol	熟人気のあるアイドル

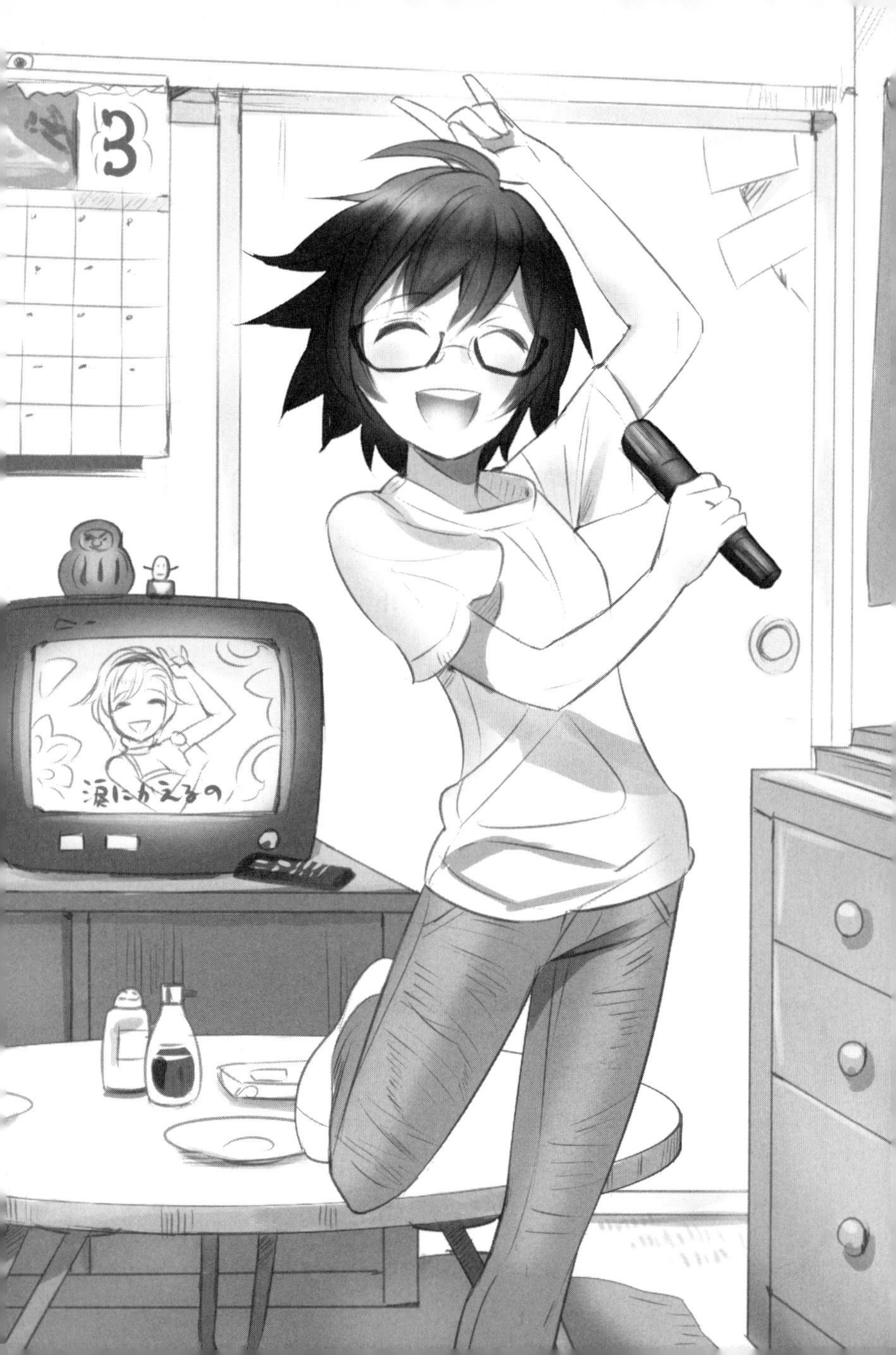
3
涙にかえるの

She was only sixteen years old, but she always had something interesting to say. Meg was fifteen years old then. She couldn't believe that a girl only one year older than her could sing and talk so well.

Although she knew it was impossible, Meg wanted to be like Momo. She sang Momo's songs and practiced dancing like Momo thousands of times. She learned most of Momo's hit numbers by heart. When she was singing and dancing like Momo, she could forget about her miserable life.

WORD LIST

□ believe	動信じる
□ although	接 ..... けれども(にも関わらず)
□ impossible	形不可能な
□ want to be 〜	熟〜になりたい
□ like 〜	前〜のような（に）
□ practice Ving	熟Vする練習をする
□ thousands of times	熟何千回も
□ most of 〜	熟〜の大部分
□ hit	名〈音楽などの〉ヒット
□ number	名〈歌などの〉1曲
□ by heart	熟そらで、暗記して
□ when	接 ..... とき
□ forget	動忘れる
	forget - forgot - forgotten
□ miserable	形惨めな、不幸な
□ life	名生活、生命、人生

MEG the Miracle Idol Vol.1
Where're Mom and Dad?

One day, her parents were busy arranging the furniture. It was so noisy that Meg decided to go out. She went to a park and spent the whole day there, reading some comic books she had found in a garbage pile.

When Meg came home, the door was unlocked, and there was no one in the house. Many pieces of furniture were gone. Meg waited for her parents, but even after nine o'clock, they hadn't come back. She was so hungry that she took out some tofu from the

---

WORD LIST

☐ arrange	動 整頓する、配置する
☐ furniture	名 家具
☐ noisy	形 騒がしい
☐ decide to V	熟 V することに決める
☐ go out	熟 外出する
☐ spend	動〈時間を〉過ごす spend - spent - spent
☐ whole day	熟 まる一日
☐ garbage	名 生ゴミ、がらくた
☐ pile	名 積み重ね、山
☐ unlocked	形 鍵のかかっていない
☐ many pieces of furniture	熟 たくさんの家具
☐ gone	形〈物が〉消失した
☐ wait for ~	熟 ~を待つ
☐ come back	戻る come - came - come
☐ take out ~	熟 ~を取り出す take - took - taken

refrigerator and ate it with soy sauce.

Although she didn't like her parents so much, she felt very lonely being alone at night in an empty house. She felt like crying. So, to cheer herself up, Meg spent time singing songs.

At about eleven o'clock, there was a knock on the door. Meg thought her parents had come back, so she opened the door. She saw a middle-aged man who looked like a gangster standing there.

To be continued

WORD LIST

- refrigerator ㊃冷蔵庫
- soy sauce ㊾醤油
- although ..... ㊊ .....けれども(にも関わらず)
- feel C ㊾ C に感じる
- lonely ㊢孤独な、寂しい
- alone ㊢たった一人で
- empty ㊢空の
- feel like Ving ㊾ V したい気がする
  feel - felt - felt
- cheer oneself up ㊾自分の気持ちを引き立てる
- spend 時間 Ving ㊾ V するのに時間を費やす
- knock ㊃ノック（の音）
- middle-aged ㊢中年の
- look like ～ ㊾～に見える
- gangster ㊃ギャング、暴力団員

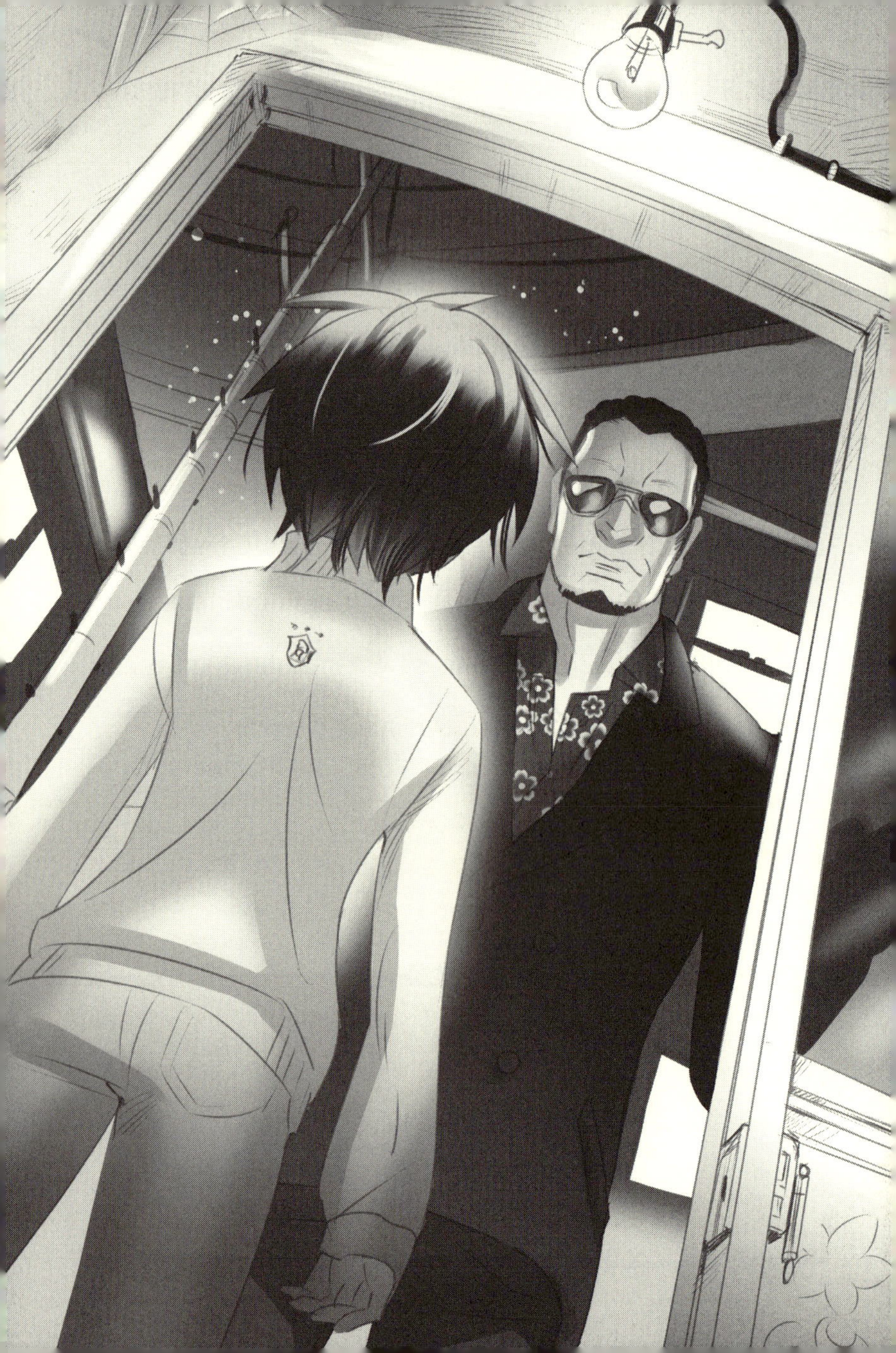

MEG
the Miracle Idol
Vol. 1
You can be a Star!

Chapter 2

-
-
-
-
-
-
-
-

The House is Gone.

The House is Gone.

"Where are your parents?" the stranger said to Meg.

Meg was a little scared. His way of talking was like a yakuza gangster's on TV dramas.

"I don't know. When I came home, they were gone," replied Meg.

"So they ran away."

"What do you mean they ran away?"

WORD LIST

□ gone	形〈物が〉消失した、出かけている
□ stranger	名見知らぬ人
□ scared	形怯えた
□ one's way of talking	熟〜の話し方
□ like 〜	前〜のような（に）
□ gangster	名ギャング、暴力団員
□ when	接 ..... とき
□ reply	動返事をする、答える
□ run away	熟逃げる　run - ran - run
□ mean	動意味する

Meg was upset. She couldn't believe her parents had done such a cruel thing to her. She didn't understand why they hadn't taken her with them. She felt very sad.

"Well, your parents couldn't pay their debts, so they ran. Now we need to take the house and the land."

"No, you can't. I live here."

"That's not my problem. My problem is that I need to collect the money I lent to your parents. Now that

WORD LIST

□ upset	形混乱した	□ debt	名借金
□ believe	動信じる	□ need to V	熟Vする必要がある
□ such	形そのような	□ land	名土地
□ cruel	形冷酷な、むごい	□ live	動住む、生きる
□ feel C	熟Cに感じる feel - felt - felt	□ problem	名問題
□ sad	形悲しい	□ collect	動徴収する、集める
□ pay	動支払う	□ lend	動貸す　lend - lent - lent

MEG the Miracle Idol Vol.1
The House is Gone.

they are gone, I have a right to this house and the land. Well, the house is too old, so I think I'll have it torn down first thing tomorrow morning, and I'll sell the land. It's perfectly legal."

"No, you can't. Then I will have nowhere to go."

"That's not my problem. Didn't you hear me? It's perfectly legal. You can go to the city office or whatever, okay?"

With that, the man was gone.

When Meg woke up the next morning, she heard

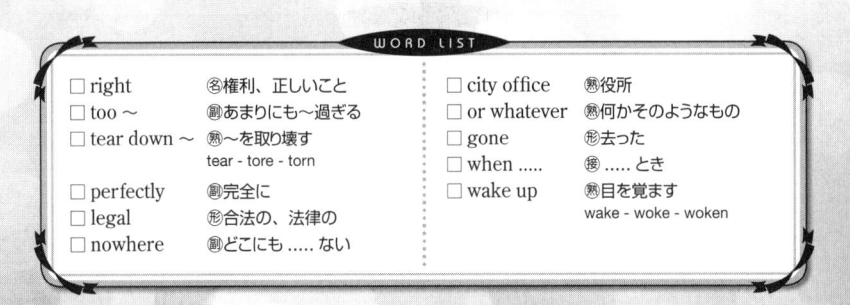

WORD LIST

- right — 名権利、正しいこと
- too ~ — 副あまりにも~過ぎる
- tear down ~ — 熟~を取り壊す
  tear - tore - torn
- perfectly — 副完全に
- legal — 形合法の、法律の
- nowhere — 副どこにも..... ない
- city office — 熟役所
- or whatever — 熟何かそのようなもの
- gone — 形去った
- when ..... — 接..... とき
- wake up — 熟目を覚ます
  wake - woke - woken

a loud noise outside. She went outside in the jersey she always wore when she slept.

It was a cloudy day in March and the morning air made her tremble a little.

There were two bulldozers and several workers. One of them said, "Okay, the girl's out. Let's start."

Then the bulldozers rolled up to the house and began tearing it down.

Meg could do nothing but watch her house smashed into rubble. She couldn't utter any words.

WORD LIST

□ loud	形〈声・音が〉大きい、うるさい	□ bulldozer	名ブルドーザー
□ noise	名音、物音	□ then	副それから
□ outside	副外へ（で）	□ roll up	熟〈車が〉乗り入れる
□ jersey	名ジャージ	□ can do nothing but V	熟ただVするしかできない
□ make O V	熟OにVさせる make - made - made	□ smash	動粉々になる
		□ rubble	名破片、がれき
□ tremble	動身震いする	□ utter	動〈言葉などを〉発する

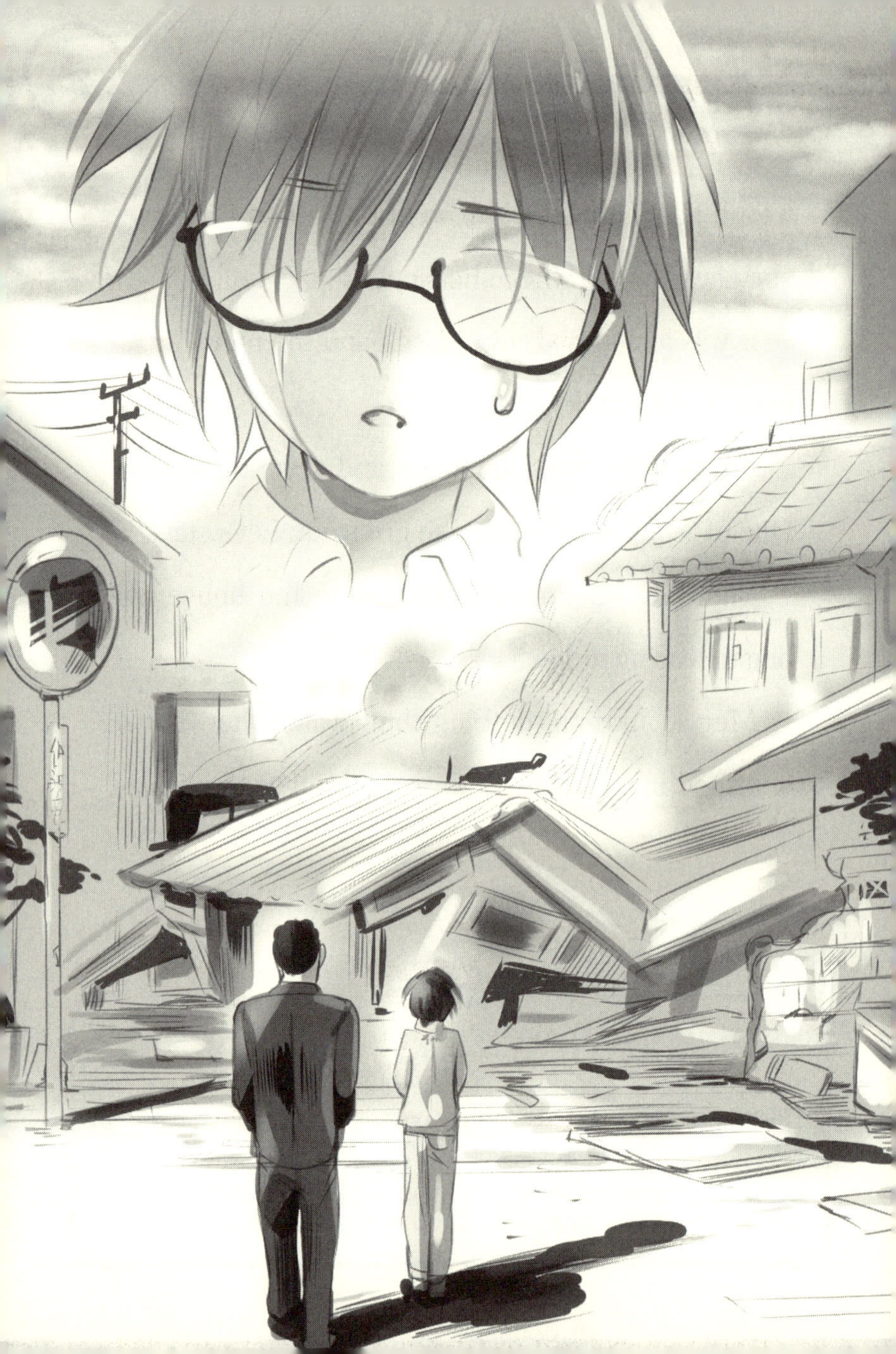

She couldn't move. Tears welled up in her eyes.

Meg felt someone patting her shoulder from behind. She turned around and saw that it was the man she had met the night before.

"Life's very cruel. You have to learn to accept that fact. This is not your fault, so don't blame yourself."

As he said that, the man gave Meg an envelope, and then he was gone.

Meg just stood there in a daze for several minutes holding the envelope. Her face was pale, and tears

WORD LIST			
☐ tear	名涙	☐ accept	動受け入れる
☐ well up	熟〈涙などが〉湧き上がる	☐ fact	名事実
☐ pat	動軽く叩く	☐ fault	名責任、落ち度
☐ from behind	熟後ろから	☐ blame	動責める
☐ turn around	熟振り向く、ぐるりと向きを変える	☐ oneself	代自分自身
		☐ envelope	名封筒
☐ life	名生活、生命、人生	☐ gone	形去った
☐ cruel	形むごい、冷酷な	☐ in a daze	熟ぼうっとして
☐ have to V	熟 V しなければならない	☐ pale	形青白い、青ざめた

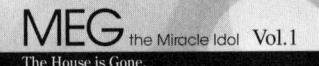

kept flowing from her eyes.

Then she opened the envelope and found it was stuffed with ten thousand yen bills.

To be continued

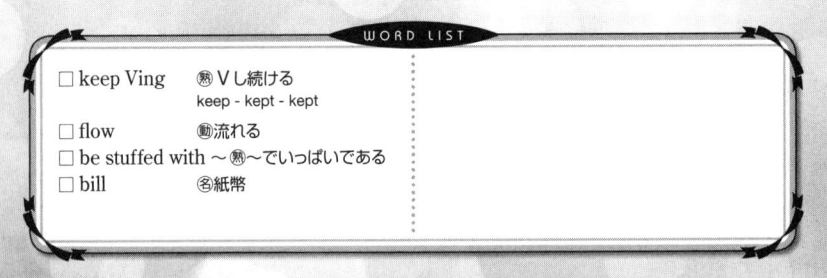

WORD LIST

- keep Ving　㊥ Vし続ける
  keep - kept - kept
- flow　㊙流れる
- be stuffed with ～　㊥～でいっぱいである
- bill　㊁紙幣

MEG
the Miracle Idol
Vol. 1
You can be a Star!

Chapter 3

Easy Homeless Life

Easy Homeless Life

Meg didn't know where to go. She was walking around downtown Tokyo. Her eyes were full of tears. When she looked up, she saw a big TV screen on a building. On the screen Momo Sakura was singing. She stopped and stood looking at the screen for several minutes.

She said to herself, "Why is the world so cruel to me? Momo and I are about the same age, but I'm

---

WORD LIST

☐ homeless	形家のない
☐ life	名生活、生命、人生
☐ walk around	熟ぶらぶら歩く、散歩する
☐ downtown	名繁華街
☐ be full of ~	熟~でいっぱいである
☐ tear	名涙
☐ when	接 ..... とき
☐ look up	熟見上げる
☐ look at ~	熟~を見る
☐ cruel	形むごい、冷酷な
☐ say to oneself	熟(心の中で) 考える、ひとりごとを言う

homeless now, and she is there on television. Well… I won't think about it any more. I need to think about how to live." She wiped away her tears.

Meg remembered the envelope the strange man had given her. Meg took out the bills from the envelope and counted them. There were fifteen of them. For Meg, that was a lot of money, but she didn't know what to do with it.

She didn't have any place to go other than the city office, but she didn't want to go there. If she went

---

WORD LIST

☐ think about ~	熟～について考える	☐ bill	名紙幣
☐ any more	熟これ以上	☐ count	動数える
☐ how to V	熟Vする方法、Vの仕方	☐ a lot of ~	熟たくさんの~
☐ live	動生きる	☐ place	名場所
☐ wipe away ~	熟～をぬぐい去る	☐ other than ~	熟～以外の
☐ remember	動思い出す、覚えている	☐ city office	名役所
☐ envelope	名封筒	☐ want to V	熟Vしたい
☐ strange	形見知らぬ、奇妙な	☐ if	接もし.....ならば
☐ take out ~	熟～を取り出す		

MEG the Miracle Idol Vol.1
Easy Homeless Life

there, she would probably be put into a home with strict rules. She didn't want to lose her freedom.

Meg decided to live by herself. She went to a store and got a tent and all the camping gear she needed. She also got some food and clothes. She spent half the money she had, but she got enough things to live by herself.

Meg set up the tent on a riverbank. She set it up under a bridge to avoid the rain. Once it was set up, the place was very cozy. There was a bathhouse and

---

WORD LIST

- probably 副 たぶん
- strict 形 厳しい
- rule 名 規則
- lose 動 失う　lose - lost - lost
- freedom 名 自由
- decide to V 熟 Vすることに決める
- by oneself 熟 独りで、独力で
- camping gear 名 キャンプ用品
- spend 動〈金を〉使う
- half 名 半分
- enough ~ to V 熟 Vするに足りる~
- set up ~ 熟 ~を設置する　set - set - set
- riverbank 名 川岸、川の土手
- avoid 動 避ける
- once ..... 接 いったん ..... すると
- cozy 形 居心地の良い
- bathhouse 名（公衆）浴場

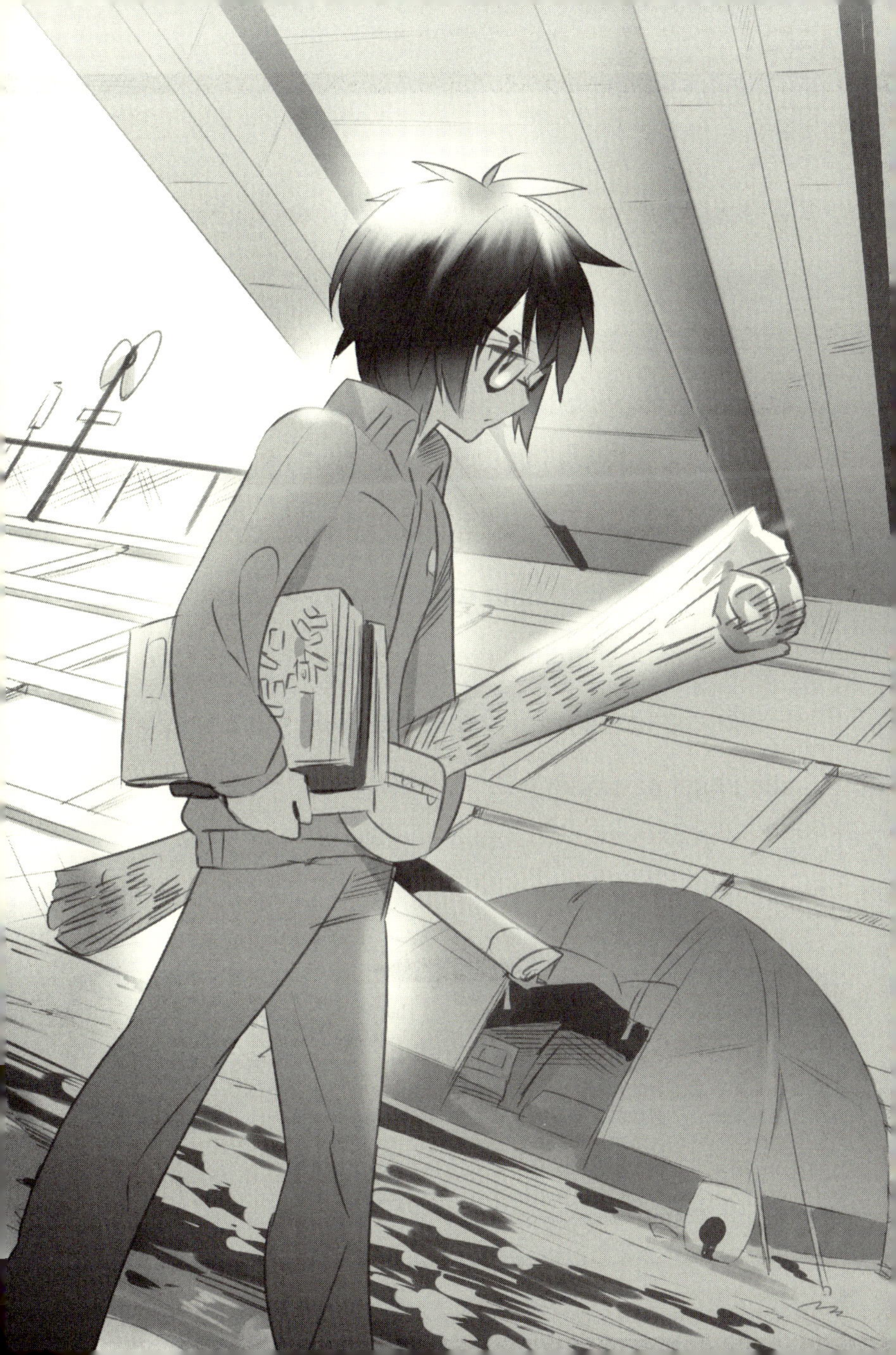

a Laundromat nearby. She had everything she needed.

She collected many comic books and magazines from garbage piles, and she bought a portable television set at a sale. She was never bored. Every day she spent hours singing and dancing on the riverside and watching television or reading manga in the tent.

Meg spent several weeks like that, but finally she ran short of money.

WORD LIST

- Laundromat ㊁コインランドリー
- nearby ㊃近くに（で）
- collect ㊁集める
- comic book ㊅マンガ本
- garbage ㊁生ゴミ、がらくた
- pile ㊁積み重ね、山
- portable ㊂携帯用の
- buy ～ at a sale ㊅～をセールで買う
  buy - bought - bought
- bored ㊂退屈した
- riverside ㊁河岸、川辺
- like ～ ㊀～のような（に）
- finally ㊃ついに
- run short of money ㊅金がなくなる
  run - ran - run

So she began collecting the change people had forgotten to pick up at vending machines and video arcades. Surprisingly, she was able to find enough for her baths and laundry. For food, Meg shoplifted bread or fruit from local stores. She knew it was a bad thing to do. She felt very guilty, but she had no choice. She never wanted to lose this freedom, so she was very careful not to be caught.

Meg liked this lifestyle. There was nobody to bully or beat her, and she could sing and dance as much as

WORD LIST

- □ change 名小銭
- □ pick up 〜 熟〜を拾い上げる
- □ vending machine 熟自動販売機
- □ video arcade 熟ゲームセンター
- □ surprisingly 副驚いたことに
- □ be able to V 熟Vできる
- □ find 動見つける
  find - found - found
- □ shoplift 動万引きをする
- □ local store 熟地元の小売店
- □ guilty 形罪の意識がある、有罪の
- □ choice 名選択
- □ catch 動捕まえる
  catch - caught - caught
- □ lifestyle 名生活様式、生き方
- □ bully 動いじめる
- □ beat 動打つ、殴る、たたく
- □ as much as ..... 熟 .....なだけ

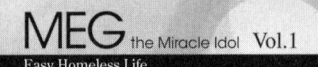

she wanted. She wished to live like this forever.

To be continued

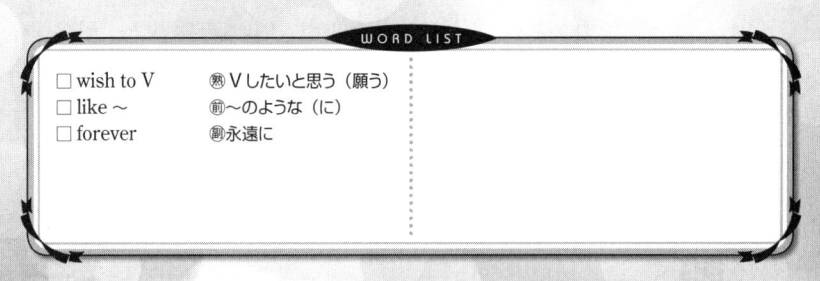

WORD LIST

- wish to V　　熟 V したいと思う（願う）
- like ~　　　前 ～のような（に）
- forever　　　副 永遠に

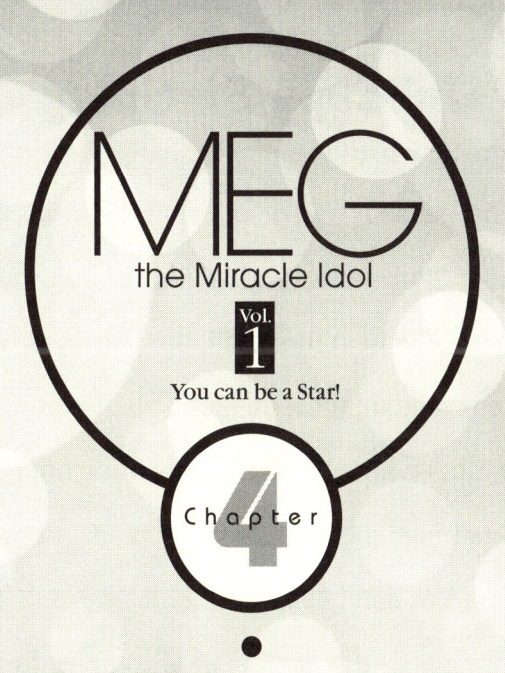

MEG the Miracle Idol

Vol. 1 — You can be a Star!

Chapter 4

Unhappy Birthday

Unhappy Birthday

Months passed and it was now September. The typhoon season came and a big typhoon hit the Tokyo area. The next morning, the river was flooded. The water came up to her tent, so she had to leave it. She didn't have time to take things out from her tent. The only thing she managed to take out was her glasses. She was in her jersey.

She watched the water swallow her tent and

WORD LIST

☐ pass	動〈時が〉過ぎる
☐ September	名9月
☐ typhoon season	熟台風の季節
☐ hit	動〈嵐が〉襲う
☐ area	名地域、地方
☐ flood	動溢れさせる、氾濫させる
☐ come up	熟近付く、達する
	come - came - come
☐ have to V	熟Vしなければならない
	have - had - had
☐ leave	動去る
☐ take out ~	熟~を持ち出す
	take - took - taken
☐ manage to V	熟なんとかVする
☐ glasses	名メガネ
☐ jersey	名ジャージ
☐ swallow	動のみ込む

everything she had. This was the second time she had seen her home go. She felt like she was watching a movie. This time no tears came to her eyes. Sadly, it was her sixteenth birthday. Meg remembered the strange man's words, "Life's very cruel." Meg thought the words were quite true... at least for her.

She spent the whole afternoon in a video arcade collecting coins. She only found one hundred yen, which was barely enough to buy a piece of bread.

In the evening, Meg was sitting and eating bread

WORD LIST

- second 形第2の
- feel like ..... 熟 ..... のような気がする
  feel - felt - felt
- tear 名涙
- sadly 副残念なことには、不幸にも
- remember 動思い出す、覚えている
- strange 形見知らぬ、奇妙な
- life 名生活、生命、人生
- cruel 形むごい、冷酷な
- quite 副まったく、とても
- true 形本当の
- at least 熟少なくとも
- whole 形全体の、まる
- coin 名硬貨
- barely 副かろうじて、やっと
- enough to V 熟 V するのに十分である
- a piece of bread 熟パン1個

MEG the Miracle Idol Vol.1
Unhappy Birthday

in a back alley. She was desperate. She thought she would have no choice but to go to the city office the next morning. She was very sad that she would have to lose her freedom.

Suddenly three drunken boys surrounded her. They looked very dangerous, with dyed hair and tattoos.

"What's a little girl like you doing here, huh? Would you like to come with us? We can teach you a lot of things, hehe…" one of the boys said.

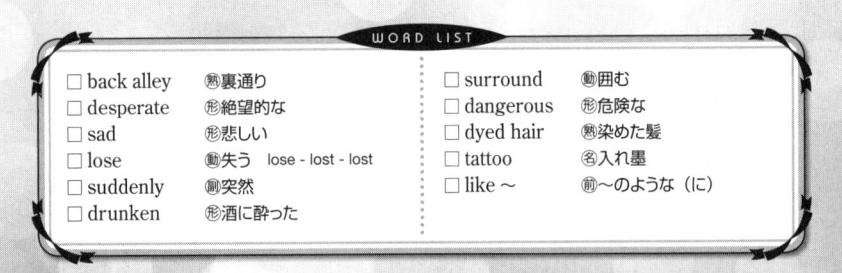

WORD LIST

- back alley 熟裏通り
- desperate 形絶望的な
- sad 形悲しい
- lose 動失う lose - lost - lost
- suddenly 副突然
- drunken 形酒に酔った
- surround 動囲む
- dangerous 形危険な
- dyed hair 熟染めた髪
- tattoo 名入れ墨
- like ～ 前～のような（に）

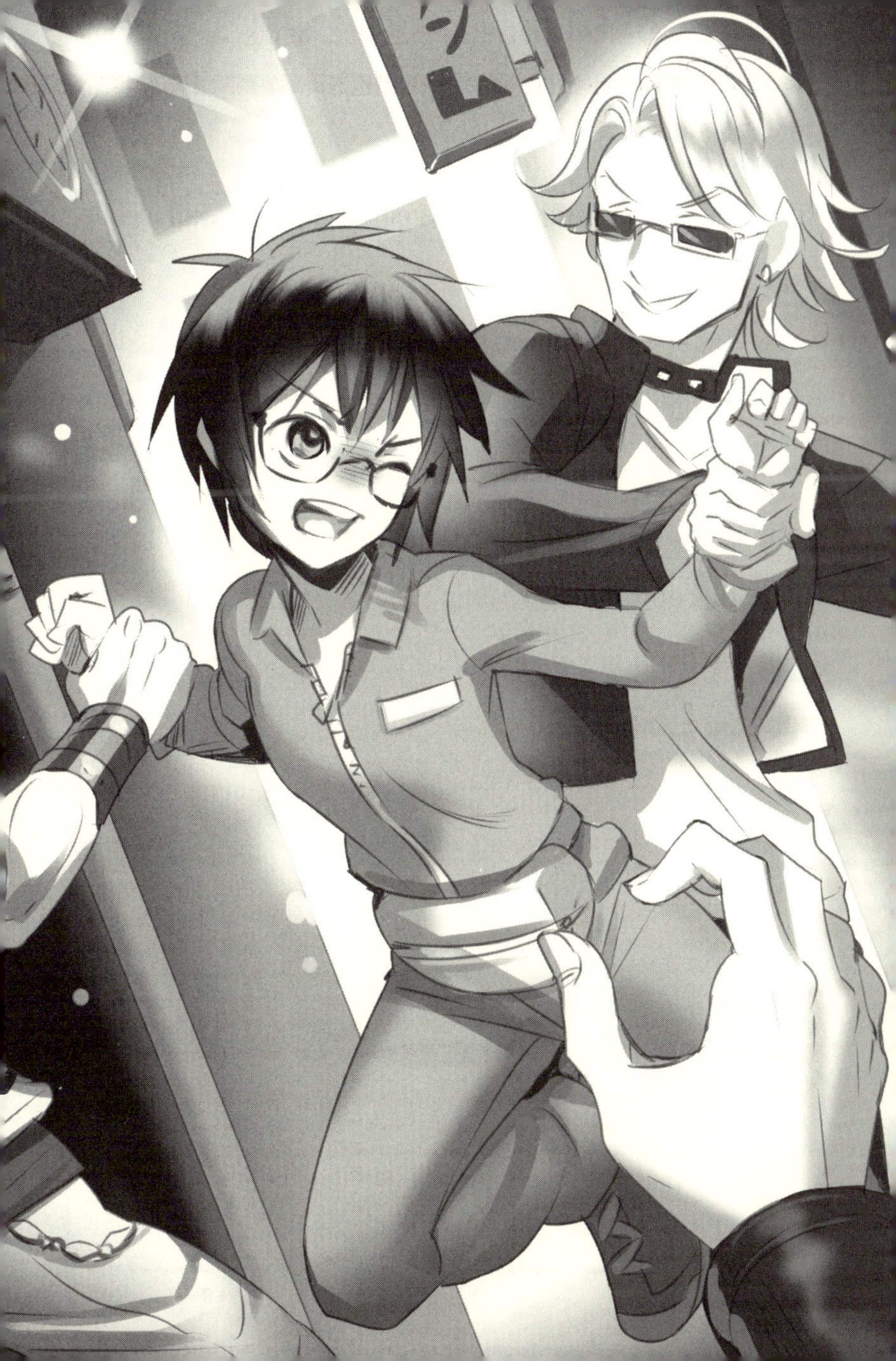

MEG the Miracle Idol Vol.1
Unhappy Birthday

"Please leave me alone. If you can't... just kill me," Meg said.

"That's no problem, but not now."

Saying that, the boy grabbed her arm.

"Stop it," Meg screamed and tried to escape, but another boy grabbed the other arm.

She continued screaming, but no one came. Tears flowed from her eyes.

To be continued

WORD LIST

☐ leave ~ alone	熟 ~をかまわずそのままにしておく
☐ kill	動〈人を〉殺す
☐ grab	動つかむ
☐ arm	名腕
☐ scream	動金切り声を出す
☐ try to V	熟 Vしようと試みる
☐ escape	動逃げる
☐ another	形もう1人の
☐ continue	動続ける
☐ flow	動流れる

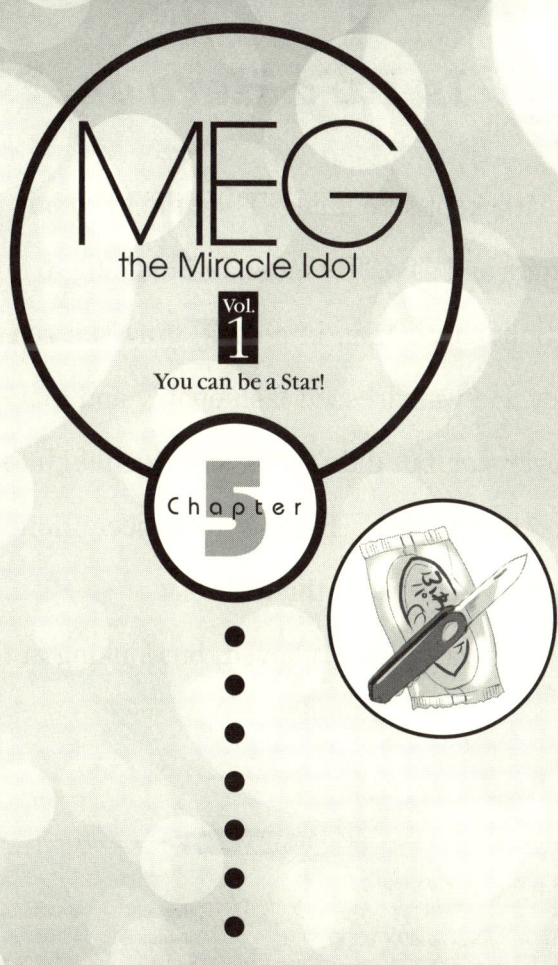

MEG
the Miracle Idol
Vol. 1
You can be a Star!

Chapter 5

Is He a Hero or ...?

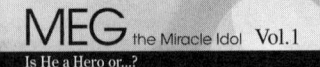

Is He a Hero or...?

Meg kept screaming. Then the third boy took out a knife and said, "Be quiet, or I'm going to hurt you."

Suddenly a man in a dark, gray suit ran into the alley. He was dressed fashionably and looked like a movie star, but didn't look strong enough to take on the young guys. His hair was nicely done and he seemed to be in his thirties.

Meg was a little relieved, but looking at the man,

WORD LIST

- keep Ving — V し続ける / keep - kept - kept
- scream — 金切り声を出す
- third — 第3の
- knife — ナイフ
- quiet — 静かな
- hurt — 傷つける、けがをさせる
- gray — 灰色の
- run into ~ — ~に駆け込む / run - ran - run
- alley — 小道、路地
- fashionably — 流行を追って、いきに
- look C — C に見える
- take on ~ — ~を相手にする
- nicely — きちんと、親切に
- seem to be C — C のように見える
- in one's thirties — 30代に
- relieve — 安心させる、取り除く

she got very anxious. She was worried that the man would be beaten up by the boys. She thought the situation might get worse.

The boys looked at him and one of them said, "Hey, if you don't want to get hurt, don't interfere. You'll get blood on your nice suit. Go away."

The man replied, "No, no. I don't want to fight you. I just want to propose a deal."

He held up his cell phone and said, "I'll pay for the girl. You leave the girl alone, and I'll pay you one

---

WORD LIST

☐ get C	熟 C になる get - got - gotten	☐ interfere	動じゃまをする
		☐ blood	名血
☐ anxious	形不安な	☐ go away	熟立ち去る、消え失せる
☐ worried	形心配した	☐ fight	動戦う
☐ beat up ～	熟～をぶちのめす、～にリンチを加える	☐ propose	動提案する
		☐ deal	名取引、契約
☐ situation	名状況	☐ hold up ～	熟～を持ち上げる hold - held - held
☐ worse	形より悪い		
☐ if	接もし ..... ならば	☐ cell phone	熟携帯電話

hundred thousand yen. How's that? My people are waiting in the car parked on the main street, and if I push this button, they will come right away. So don't get any ideas."

He was very convincing, and he looked very important. The boys just listened to him. Besides, one hundred thousand yen sounded very attractive to them.

"Show us the money first," one of the boys said.

The man took out his wallet and threw it to the

WORD LIST

- park 動駐車する（させる）
- main street 熟大通り
- push 動押す
- button 名ボタン
- right away 熟すぐに
- convincing 形人を納得させる
- important 形地位の高い、重要な
- listen to ～ 熟～に耳を傾ける
- besides 副その上、さらに
- sound C 熟Cに聞こえる
- attractive 形魅力的な
- first 副最初に
- take out ～ 熟～を取り出す
- wallet 名財布
- throw 動投げる
  throw - threw - thrown

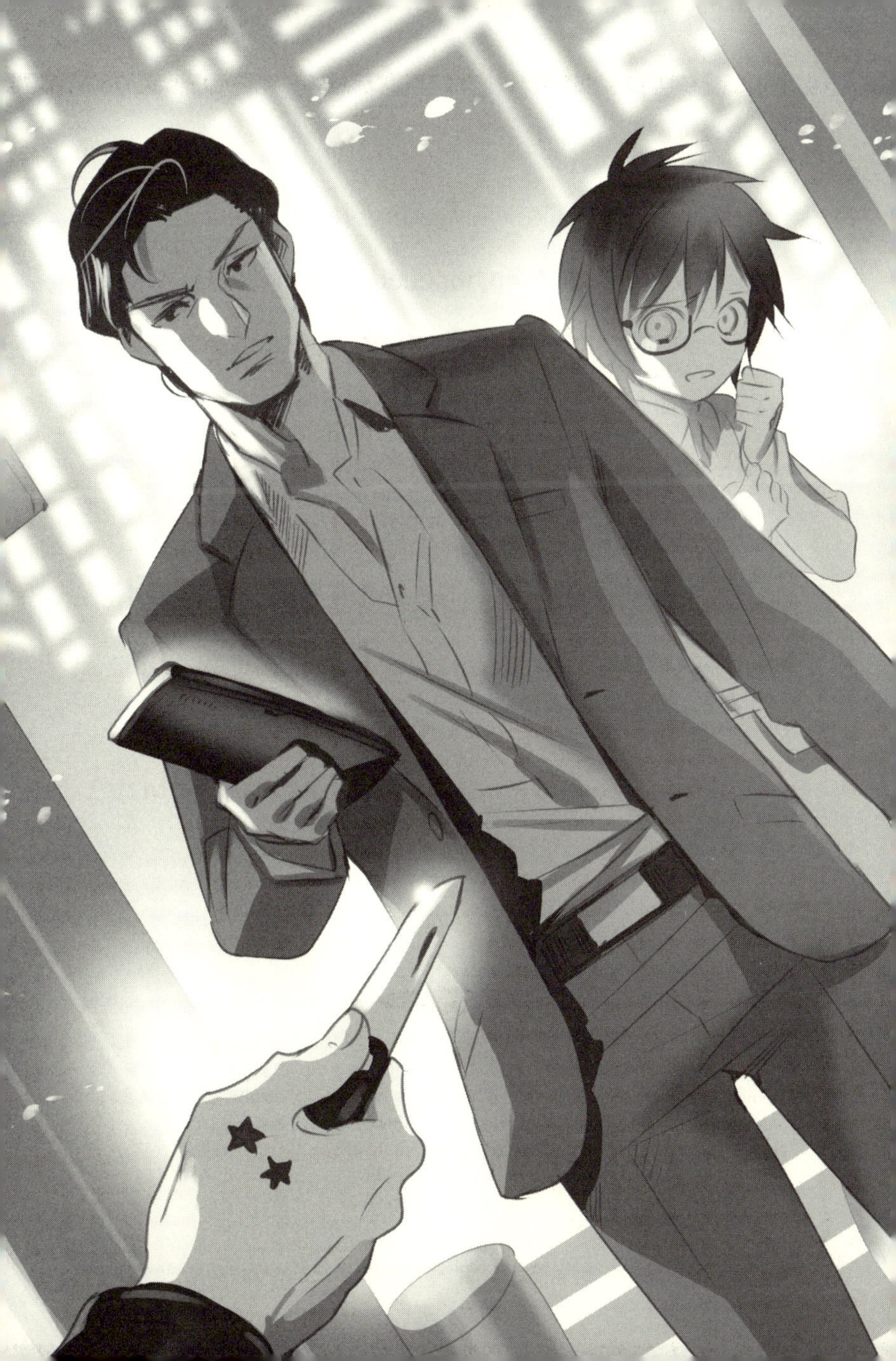

boys and said, "Take everything. It's all yours."

A boy picked it up, opened it and said, "Wow! There is more than one hundred thousand yen here! It's almost two hundred thousand yen!"

Another boy said to Meg, "You're a lucky girl. Be nice to that old man, hehe."

Meg gave a sigh of relief and felt thankful to the man, but also felt sorry because he lost a lot of money by helping her.

After the boys were gone, the man said to Meg,

WORD LIST

□ pick up ~	熟 ~を拾い上げる
□ more than ~	熟 ~よりも多い
□ almost	副 大体、ほとんど
□ another	形 もう1人の
□ give a sigh of relief	熟 ほっとしてため息をつく
□ feel C	熟 Cに感じる (feel - felt - felt)
□ thankful to ~	熟 ~に感謝している
□ also	副 また
□ sorry	形 気の毒で、すまなく思って
□ because	接 ..... なので
□ a lot of ~	熟 たくさんの~
□ help	動 助ける
□ gone	形 去った

"Don't make your parents worried any more. Go home, girl."

"Thank you for helping me, but I have no home. I have nowhere to go," Meg said crying. "I lost everything. My parents, my home and all my money. I don't know what to do."

"All right. Let me give you something to drink to calm you down, and then let's think about what to do. Let's go."

Meg followed him and found a big, black Lexus

WORD LIST

☐ make OC	熟 O を C にする	☐ let ～ V	熟 ～に V させる
☐ any more	熟 これ以上	☐ something to drink	熟 何か飲む物
☐ thank you for ～	熟 ～してくれてありがとう	☐ calm ～ down	熟 ～を落ち着かせる
☐ nowhere	副 どこにも..... ない	☐ then	副 それから
☐ lose	動 失う lose - lost - lost	☐ think about ～	熟 ～について考える
☐ everything	代 何もかも	☐ follow	動 後について行く、従う、続く

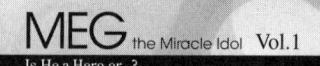

parked on the main street.

There was no one in the car.

To be continued

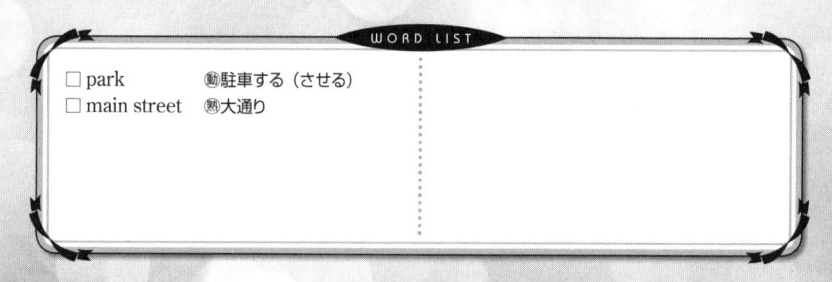

WORD LIST

- park　　　　　動駐車する（させる）
- main street　　熟大通り

MEG
the Miracle Idol
Vol. 1
You can be a Star!

Chapter 6

Won't You be an Idol?

Won't You be an Idol?

Meg and the man got into the car. The man sat in the driver's seat, and Meg sat in the passenger seat beside him.

She said, "Where are your people? You were bluffing?"

"Yeah, of course. Those guys never knew."

He started the engine.

"Where are we going? Who are you?" Meg asked.

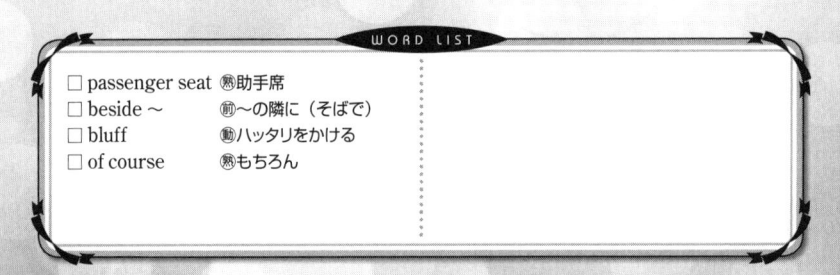

WORD LIST

- passenger seat　熟 助手席
- beside 〜　　　前 〜の隣に（そばで）
- bluff　　　　　動 ハッタリをかける
- of course　　　熟 もちろん

"Well, I own a company. I'll take you to my office. You can stay there for the night."

"Huh? Are you bluffing again?"

"No. It's true. We are going to Roppongi, where my office is. Have some tea if you want."

Meg knew it was dangerous to trust this man, but she thought it was better than sleeping on the street. Besides, he didn't look like a bad person to Meg, and she kind of liked him.

He handed a can of green tea to Meg and started

WORD LIST

□ own	動所有する	□ besides	副その上、さらに
□ true	形本当の	□ look like ~	熟～に見える
□ if	接もし ..... ならば	□ kind of	熟ある程度、どちらかというと
□ dangerous	形危険な	□ hand	動手渡す
□ trust	動信用する	□ a can of green tea	熟缶入りの緑茶
□ be better than ~	熟～よりはましである		

driving. Meg opened the can and drank some tea. She felt everything catch up with her and got sleepy.

"You must be tired. Have a nap. It'll take us about thirty minutes."

Meg's eyes closed.

When she opened her eyes, she saw a huge, beautiful skyscraper in front of her. They were at Roppongi Hills, in one of the most luxurious districts in Tokyo. The car went into the basement of the building.

WORD LIST

□ feel O V	熟 O が V するのを感じる feel - felt - felt
□ catch up with ~	熟 ~に追いつく
□ get C	熟 C になる
□ sleepy	形 眠い
□ tired	形 疲れた
□ nap	名 昼寝、うたた寝
□ skyscraper	名 超高層ビル
□ in front of ~	熟 ~の前に
□ luxurious	形 贅沢な、豪華な
□ district	名 地区
□ basement	名 地階

Meg thought that the man really must be a company owner.

After parking the car, they took the elevator to the 32nd floor. Just outside the elevator, there was a reception desk with a sign saying "Tokyo Productions." There were two receptionists behind the counter, and there was a huge digital display over their heads. The display showed the pictures of many famous TV personalities, including Momo Sakura. It was a talent agency. Considering the faces of the

---

WORD LIST

□ really	副 本当に	□ behind ~	前 ~の後ろに
□ park	動 駐車する（させる）	□ counter	名 カウンター
□ take the elevator	熟 エレベーターに乗る	□ huge	形 巨大な
□ outside ~	前 ~の外側に	□ TV personality	熟 テレビタレント
□ reception desk	熟 受付カウンター	□ including ~	前 ~を含めて
□ sign	名 看板、符号	□ talent agency	熟 芸能プロダクション
□ receptionist	名 受付係	□ considering ~	前 ~を考えると

ME
Won't Yo

stars shown on the screen, Meg thought it must be a very famous one.

The receptionists bowed to the man and said, "Welcome back, Mr. Fuyumoto."

They went into a room and sat on a sofa.

"Who are you?" Meg asked.

"I said I'm a company owner. I own this talent agency."

"You mean you represent Momo Sakura and all those stars."

WORD LIST

- bow 動〈挨拶の印として〉お辞儀をする
- mean 動意味する
- represent 動代表する

Meg felt her heart beating faster. She was excited to know that she was so close to the world she had dreamed of for a very long time. She felt that finally something nice had happened in her life.

"That's right, but that doesn't have anything to do with you. You can stay here tonight, but I will take you to the city office tomorrow morning... Hey, take your glasses off."

Mr. Fuyumoto's face was very serious. He was looking intently at Meg.

WORD LIST

- feel O Ving 熟 O が V しているのを感じる feel - felt - felt
- beat 動〈心臓が〉鼓動する
- faster 形 fast（速く）の比較級
- excited 形 興奮した
- so 副 とても
- dream of ~ 熟 ~を夢見る
- for a long time 熟 長い間
- finally 副 ついに
- not have anything to do with ~ 熟 ~とは全く関係がない
- city office 熟 役所
- take ~ off 熟〈メガネなど〉を外す、〈衣服〉を脱ぐ take - took - taken
- serious 形 本気の
- glasses 名 メガネ
- intently 副 熱心に

"Why?"

"Just do it, and stand up."

"Why?"

"Just do as I say."

Meg stood up. Mr. Fuyumoto gazed closely at Meg. He thought for a moment and said to Meg, "Hey, just for fun, do you want to be an idol for a day? You had a bad day. I feel like making up for it. What do you say to that? It doesn't mean you will be a real idol. It's just a taste."

To be continued

WORD LIST

☐ stand up	熟立ち上がる stand - stood - stood	☐ want to V	熟 Vしたい
☐ gaze	動凝視する	☐ feel like Ving	熟 Vしたい気がする feel - felt - felt
☐ closely	副綿密に、細かく注意して	☐ make up for ～	熟 ～の埋め合わせをする
☐ for a moment	熟少しの間	☐ real	形本物の、本当の
☐ fun	名楽しみ、ふざけ	☐ taste	名経験、試食、味

MEG the Miracle Idol

MEG
the Miracle Idol
Vol. 1
You can be a Star!

Chapter 7

The Transformation

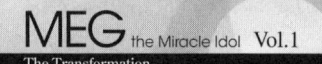

The Transformation

Meg heard a knock on the door and woke up. She was still in the jersey she had worn the day before. Her hair was messy as always. She wondered where she was and remembered she was in an office at Mr. Fuyumoto's company. She got out from under the blanket and said, "Okay, wait a moment."

She remembered what Mr. Fuyumoto said the day before. She would be a one-day idol. Her heart began

WORD LIST			
☐ wake up	熟 目を覚ます wake - woke - woken	☐ messy	形 ボサボサの、散らかった
		☐ as always	熟 いつものように
☐ still	副 まだ	☐ wonder	動 かしらと思う
☐ jersey	名 ジャージ	☐ remember	動 思い出す、覚えている
☐ wear	動 身につける wear - wore - worn	☐ blanket	名 毛布
		☐ wait a moment	熟 少しの間待つ

to beat faster. She felt very nervous, but at the same time she was very excited, thinking that she was in the same world as Momo Sakura and other top stars.

When she put on her glasses and opened the door, she saw a young woman there. She was very fashionable. She said to Meg, "I'm a stylist. Mr. Fuyumoto asked me to prepare you for today's events. Please come with me." It was only seven o'clock.

Meg followed her, and they went to a hotel room,

WORD LIST

- beat 動〈心臓が〉鼓動する
- faster 副 fast（速く）の比較級
- feel C 熟 C に感じる
  feel - felt - felt
- nervous 形緊張して、神経質な
- at the same time 熟同時に
- excited 形興奮した
- when ..... 接 ..... とき
- put on ~ 熟〈メガネ〉をかける
- glasses 名メガネ
- fashionable 形流行の
- stylist 名〈服などの〉スタイリスト
- prepare 動用意する、準備する
- event 名行事、イベント
- follow 動後について行く

also in Roppongi Hills. Meg was asked to take a shower, and then she changed into the clothes which had been prepared for her. They were a little tight and uncomfortable, but looked very good.

The dress looked like a school girl's uniform, but had orange pinstripes and metal decorations. The skirt was a little short. The dress was very tight around the waist to emphasize her bodyline.

Then Meg was taken to a beauty parlor, where she met a handsome hair stylist who said that Mr.

WORD LIST

□ also	副また	□ look like ～	熟～に見える
□ take a shower	熟シャワーを浴びる	□ uniform	名制服
□ then	副それから	□ pinstripe	名細縞
□ change into ～	熟～に着替える	□ metal	名金属
□ clothes	名衣服	□ decoration	名装飾、勲章
□ tight	形きつい	□ waist	名腰（のくびれ）
□ uncomfortable	形心地良くない	□ emphasize	動強調する
□ look C	熟Cに見える	□ beauty parlor	熟美容室

Fuyumoto had asked him to cut, dye, and style her hair. When they were finished, it was already ten o'clock. She looked at herself in the mirror, but without glasses she couldn't see well. She put on her glasses and was surprised to find herself looking completely different from the homeless girl she had been before. Her hair had been dyed brown and had big curls. She looked like the kind of rich, fashionable teenage girls often seen in Roppongi Hills.

She was taken to the hotel room again, where she

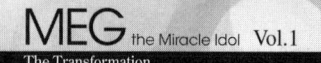

met a make-up artist. He looked like a man, but talked like a girl. Meg thought he must like other men.

It was a strange feeling for Meg to have a person doing make-up just for her for such a long time. She had never been treated nicely like this before. She felt a little sorry for the man because she felt she was not worthy.

After half an hour, he finished her make-up. Now, Meg was a completely different girl from before.

WORD LIST

- like ~ 前〜のような（に）
- strange 形不思議な、奇妙な
- treat 動扱う
- nicely 副よく、親切に
- sorry 形すまなく思って、気の毒で
- worthy 形価値がある
- half an hour 熟半時間、30分

When she put on her glasses and saw herself in the mirror, she was stunned. She looked like a real idol. She was as pretty as Momo Sakura, the super idol. She was way more beautiful than the typical pop stars on variety shows. She looked special.

Mr. Fuyumoto came into the room, and when he saw her said, "Wow! I was right. Look at you! I found a diamond!"

To be continued

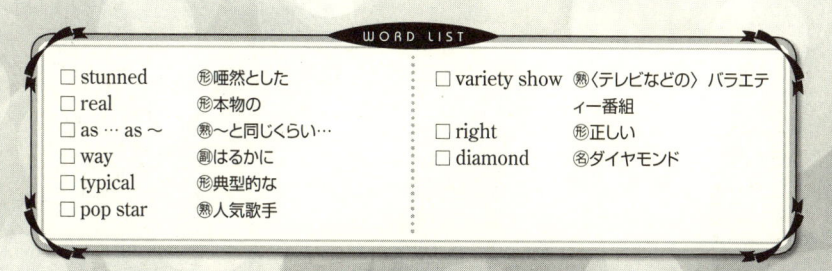

WORD LIST

- stunned 形 唖然とした
- real 形 本物の
- as … as ~ 熟 ~と同じくらい…
- way 副 はるかに
- typical 形 典型的な
- pop star 熟 人気歌手
- variety show 熟 〈テレビなどの〉バラエティー番組
- right 形 正しい
- diamond 名 ダイヤモンド

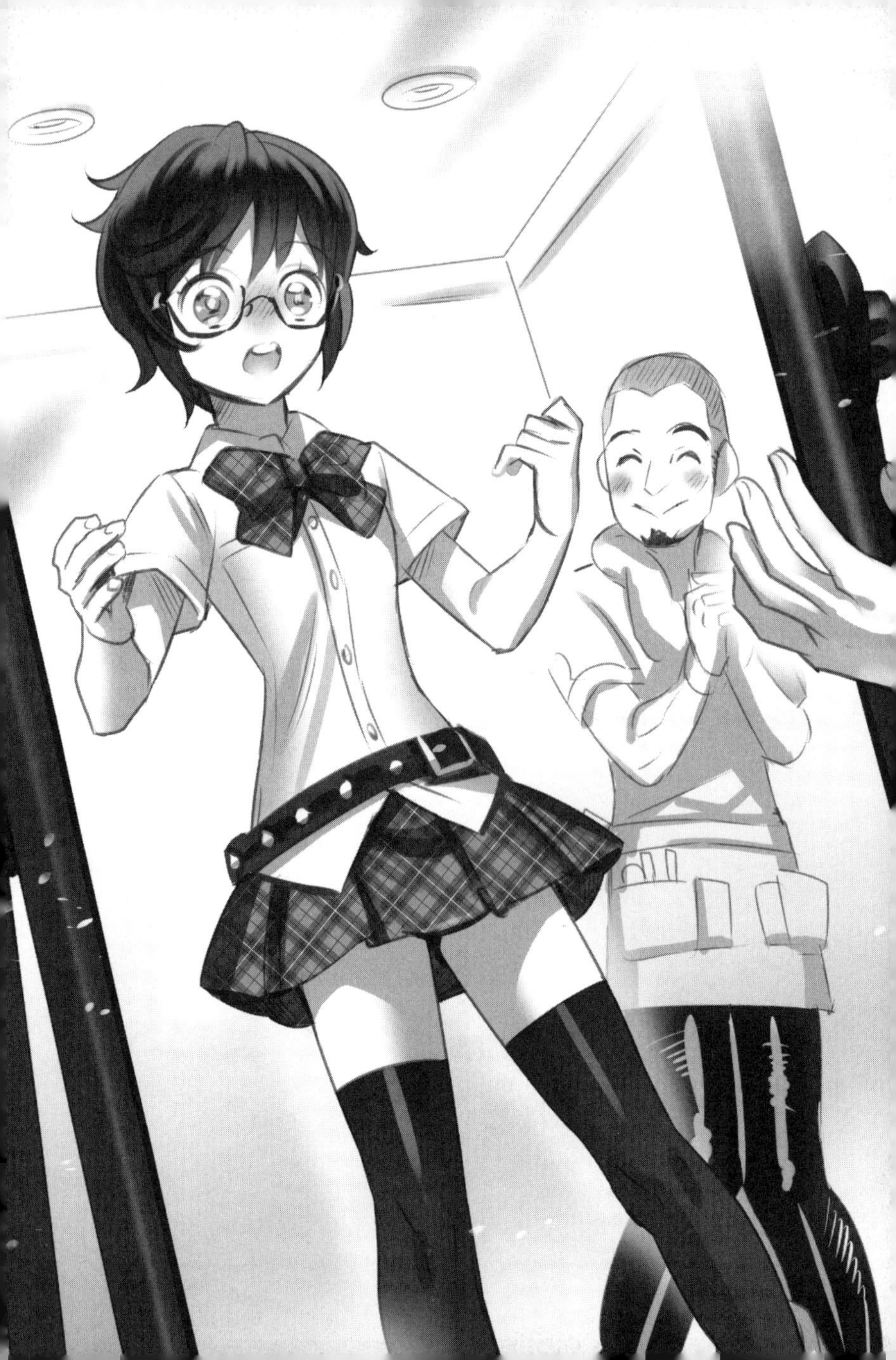

MEG
the Miracle Idol

Vol. 1

You can be a Star!

Chapter 8

Can You Sing a Song?

Can You Sing a Song?

Meg couldn't believe Mr. Fuyumoto's words.

"Diamond? Me?"

She was very glad. This was the first time anybody had praised her or appreciated her existence. It gave her self-confidence, which made her eyes shine even more and added to her exceptional beauty.

"What's your name?" Mr. Fuyumoto asked Meg.

"Meg. Meg Suzuki."

WORD LIST

☐ believe	動信じる
☐ diamond	名ダイヤモンド
☐ glad	形嬉しく思う
☐ praise	動褒める
☐ appreciate	動正しく理解する、価値を認める、ありがたく思う
☐ existence	名存在
☐ self-confidence	名自信
☐ make O V	熟OにVさせる
☐ shine	動輝く、いきいきする
☐ even	副さらに（比較級の強調）
☐ add to ~	熟~を増す
☐ exceptional	形並外れた

"All right... 'Meg' is good, but you should lose the 'Suzuki'."

"What are you talking about?"

"Your stage name. 'Suzuki' is too common. So I think just 'Meg' might be a good idea."

"Okay, I don't like my family name anyway. Besides, I don't have a family anymore. I want to be called just 'Meg'."

"Right. Then your stage name is 'Meg'. Done. And... How well can you sing?"

WORD LIST

☐ lose	動失う、なくす	☐ anyway	副いずれにせよ、ともかく
☐ talk about ~	熟～について話す	☐ call	動呼ぶ、電話をする
☐ stage name	熟〈役者の〉芸名	☐ besides	副その上
☐ too ~	副あまりにも～過ぎる	☐ anymore	副もはや
☐ common	形ありふれた、共通の	☐ want to V	熟 V したい
☐ so	接だから	☐ then	副それなら、それじゃあ

"I don't know, but I can sing many of Momo Sakura's songs. I sing them all the time, so I know the lyrics by heart. I can even dance like her. Why?"

"Well, you might have to sing today."

Meg was stunned to hear that.

"What? Today? Sing? In public? No! I can't. I'm not that good. My singing is totally average."

"That's okay. Average is fine. They like that in a singer. Can you sing 'Happy Tears'?"

'Happy Tears' was an old song from the sixties,

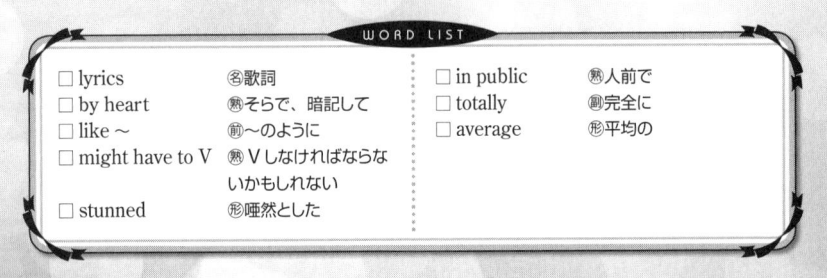

WORD LIST

☐ lyrics	名歌詞	☐ in public	熟人前で
☐ by heart	熟そらで、暗記して	☐ totally	副完全に
☐ like ~	前~のように	☐ average	形平均の
☐ might have to V	熟Vしなければならないかもしれない		
☐ stunned	形唖然とした		

which had been covered by many artists, including Momo Sakura. It was a typical pop song with a simple melody. For a Momo Sakura number, it was not that big a hit.

"Yes... but..." Meg looked nervous.

"Sing."

"Here?"

"Yes. Do it."

Meg took her glasses off. Then everything was blurry, and she didn't feel so nervous anymore. She began singing. She wasn't that great, but good enough to sing in public. Mr. Fuyumoto was impressed.

"Yes! You're pop idol material. Let's go," Mr. Fuyumoto said.

"Where?" Meg asked.

"I'm going to take you to the perfect place for your one-day debut—Akihabara."

To be continued

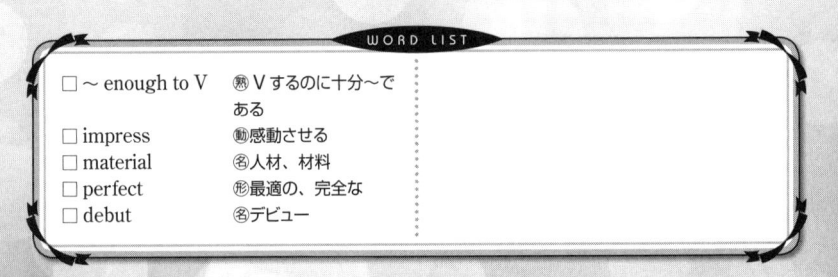

WORD LIST

☐ ~ enough to V	熟 V するのに十分~である
☐ impress	動 感動させる
☐ material	名 人材、材料
☐ perfect	形 最適の、完全な
☐ debut	名 デビュー

MEG the Miracle Idol

MEG the Miracle Idol

Vol. 1

You can be a Star!

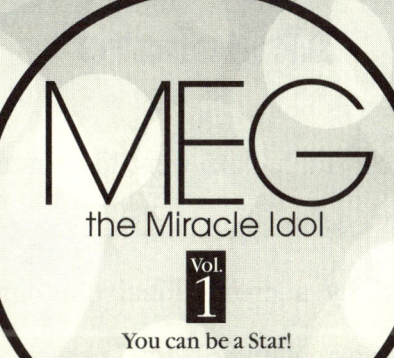

Chapter 2

Akihabara

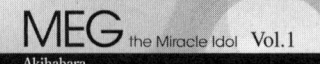

Akihabara

Meg and Mr. Fuyumoto went to a photo studio in Roppongi Hills. Meg spent about an hour having her picture taken by a professional photographer. He looked like a normal middle-aged person, but he was very funny. He taught Meg how to pose for the camera. He was always talking to Meg as he took the pictures, so she could relax. Meg liked him. She wished she had a father like him.

WORD LIST

□ spend	動〈時間を〉過ごす spend - spent - spent	□ funny	形面白い
□ have a picture taken	熟写真を撮ってもらう	□ how to V	熟 V する方法、V の仕方
□ professional	形プロの	□ pose	動ポーズをとる
□ photographer	名カメラマン	□ talk to ~	熟~に話しかける
□ look like ~	熟~に見える	□ take the pictures	熟写真を撮る
□ normal	形普通の、標準の	□ relax	動くつろぐ、リラックスする
□ middle-aged	形中年の	□ wish	動 ..... であればいいのだがと思う
		□ like ~	前~のような

Then Meg and Mr. Fuyumoto went to the parking lot and got into the big, black Lexus. A woman in a navy suit and the driver were already in the car. The woman was busily making calls and had a computer on her lap. Meg heard the woman say her name, "Meg", a lot of times in her conversation. Meg and Mr. Fuyumoto sat in the back seat, and the car started.

After about half an hour, they arrived in Akihabara. It was four o'clock in the afternoon. It was clear but

WORD LIST

- then　副それから
- parking lot　熟駐車場
- navy suit　熟濃紺色のスーツ
- already　副すでに
- busily　副忙しく
- make a call　熟電話をかける
- lap　名膝
- a lot of times　熟何回も
- conversation　名会話
- half an hour　熟半時間、30分

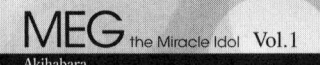

not so hot for a September day.

Akihabara is sometimes called the mecca of anime and pop idols. A lot of boys who love anime and pop stars go there to buy anime-related items and albums by their favorite artists or idol photo books. They also visit maid cafes, where young girls in maid uniforms serve drinks and chat with customers. A lot of girls who dream of being a pop star in the future work in maid cafes.

It was a Saturday. Meg could see through the car

WORD LIST

- mecca — 名メッカ、中心地
- anime — 名アニメ
- anime-related item — 熟アニメに関係ある品物
- album — 名〈レコード、CDの〉全集、アルバム
- favorite — 形お気に入りの
- also — 副また
- maid cafe — 熟メイドカフェ
- uniform — 名制服
- serve — 動〈食べ物を〉出す、提供する
- chat with ~ — 熟~と談笑する
- customer — 名顧客、常連
- dream of ~ — 熟~を夢見る
- in the future — 熟将来は
- Saturday — 名土曜日
- through ~ — 前~を通して

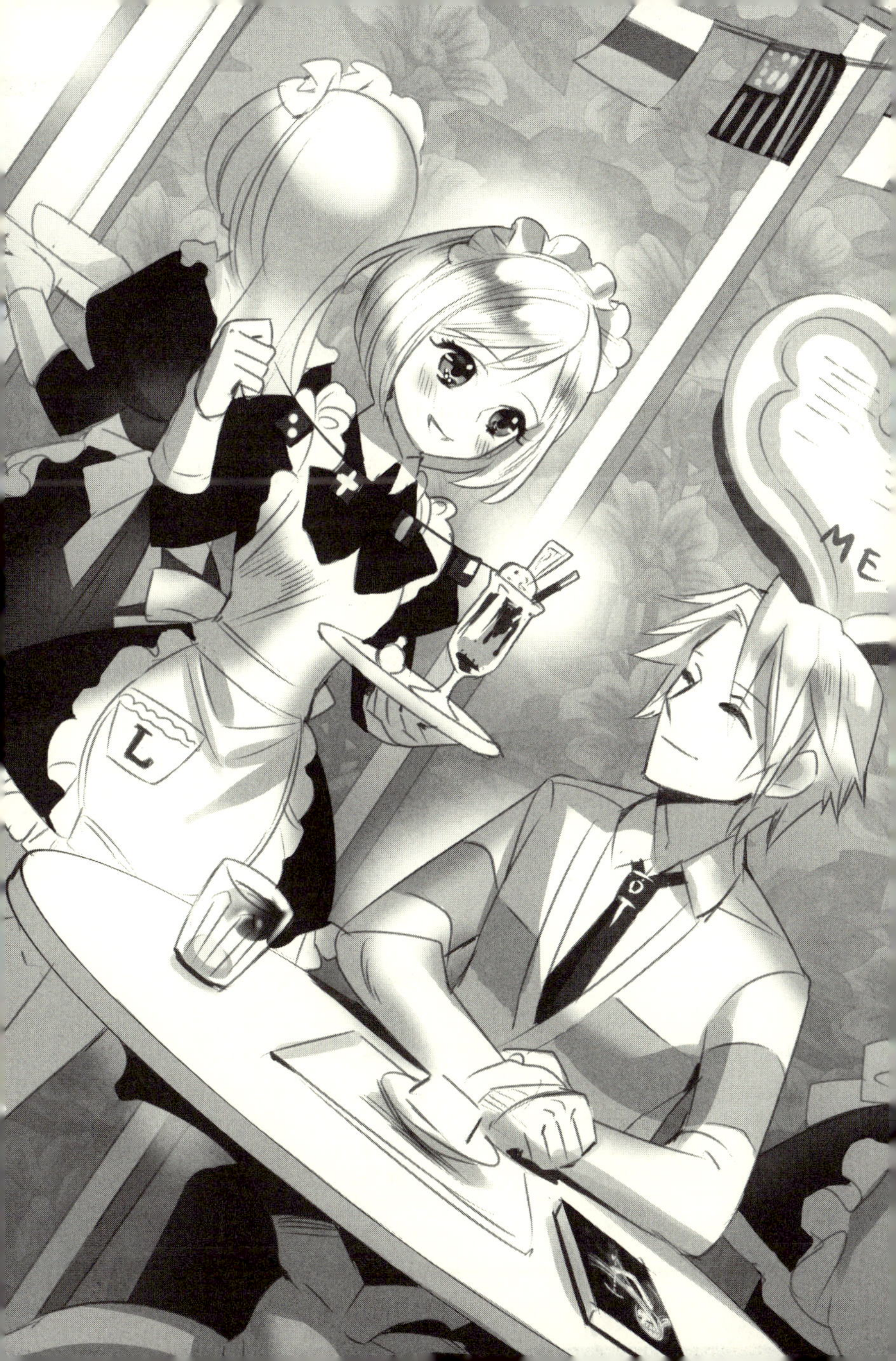
ME

windows that the streets were packed with young boys.

Mr. Fuyumoto said to the woman, "Now, Miss Sakai, give her the coat and the mask."

She gave a gray coat and a white flu mask to Meg.

"Wear them, and don't take off your glasses," Mr. Fuyumoto said to Meg.

Meg wore them and the woman got out of the car and opened the door for Meg. Meg got out onto a crowded street.

WORD LIST

- be packed with ~ 熟〜で混んでいる
- gray 形灰色の
- coat 名コート
- white flu mask 熟白いインフルエンザ予防用マスク
- wear 動身につける
- take ~ off 熟〈メガネ〉を外す、〈衣服〉を脱ぐ
- glasses 名メガネ
- get out of ~ 熟〜から降りる
- crowded 形混み合った

Chapter 9

They walked for about one hundred meters and came to the back door of a four-story building. The woman opened the door, and Meg heard loud music and cheers. They went into the building and into a very small locker room.

Mr. Fuyumoto said to Meg, "This is the idol cafe I own. You are going to make your one-day debut here. Take off your coat, mask, and your glasses. This woman is your manager for the day, Miss Sakai. If there is anything you don't know, ask her."

WORD LIST

- story 名階
- loud 形〈声・音が〉大きい
- cheer 名歓呼、喝采
- own 動所有する
- debut 名デビュー
- if ..... 接もし ..... ならば

"You go on at five o'clock. You will talk with the MC for about five minutes and sing a song, and again you will talk with him for about five minutes. Then your turn is over. Do you understand?"

"Yes... but what will I talk about?" Meg was worried.

"Your hobbies and stuff. Don't worry. Just try to smile all the time. Okay? Smile."

Meg was very nervous, but Miss Sakai was quite businesslike and sounded very reliable, which

WORD LIST			
☐ MC	⑧司会者	☐ nervous	⑱緊張して、神経質な
☐ turn	⑧番、回転	☐ quite	⑩まったく、とても
☐ over	⑩終わって	☐ businesslike	⑱事務的な
☐ and stuff	⑲～など	☐ sound C	⑲Cに聞こえる
☐ try to V	⑲Vしようと試みる	☐ reliable	⑱信頼できる
☐ smile	⑩微笑む		

relaxed Meg.

Five o'clock came. The MC said to about one hundred customers sitting in the huge cafe, "Now I'd like to introduce to you all a new star, Meg."

"Now go," Miss Sakai said and pushed Meg out, and Meg climbed up on stage. The crowd cheered.

To be continued

WORD LIST

- □ huge ㊫巨大な
- □ would like to V ㊾Vしたい
- □ introduce to A B ㊾AにBを紹介する
- □ climb up ㊾登る、上がる
- □ stage ㊇舞台
- □ crowd ㊇群衆

MEG the Miracle Idol

Just Keep Smiling!

Meg couldn't see her audience well because she was not wearing her glasses and the lights were too bright, but she could tell that there were over one hundred people cheering for her.

She ran toward the MC, but tripped on a microphone cable on the stage and fell. She fell flat on her face. The crowd froze for a moment, but as Meg rose to her feet, they began cheering again.

WORD LIST

☐ audience	名聴衆
☐ wear	動〈メガネを〉かける
☐ light	名明かり、光
☐ too ~	副あまりにも~過ぎる
☐ bright	形輝いている
☐ cheer	動喝采する
☐ toward ~	前~の方へ
☐ trip on ~	熟~につまずく
☐ fall	動転ぶ、落ちる、倒れる
	fall - fell - fallen
☐ fall flat on one's face	熟うつ伏せにばったり倒れる
☐ crowd	名群衆
☐ freeze	動動けなくなる、凍る
	freeze - froze - frozen
☐ for a moment	熟少しの間
☐ rise to one's feet	熟立ち上がる

MEG
the Miracle Idol
Vol. 1
You can be a Star!

Chapter 10

Just Keep Smiling!

Meg was very upset that she made such a silly appearance, but she braced herself up not to show her nervousness on her face.

"Are you all right, Meg?" asked the MC.

"Yes, no problem. Thank you for asking," she answered smiling, but her nose was bleeding a little.

"Are you sure? Your nose is bleeding. Can you go on?"

"Oh, is it?" She took out a handkerchief and wiped the blood off, and said smiling, "I'm okay. I'm okay.

WORD LIST

☐ upset	形混乱した	☐ bleed	動出血する
☐ silly	形愚かな	☐ sure	形確信して、確かな
☐ appearance	名出現、出演	☐ go on	熟続ける、進み続ける
☐ brace oneself up	熟気持ちを引きしめる	☐ take out ～	熟～を取り出す、持ち出す
☐ nervousness	名神経質、臆病	☐ handkerchief	名ハンカチ
☐ thank you for ～	熟～してくれてありがとう	☐ wipe ～ off	熟～を拭き取る
☐ nose	名鼻	☐ blood	名血

Let's go on."

"Wow, Meg, you're a real professional already. Doesn't that hurt?"

"No, no. My father beat me and my mother all the time when I was a kid. This is nothing compared to that." She never forgot Miss Sakai's advice to keep smiling when she talked.

"Okay... anyway... Meg... Your name is just 'Meg'. Just your first name. I think it's cool. It's like 'Jiro' the baseball star. Did you pick your stage name yourself?"

WORD LIST

□ professional	名プロ	□ advice	名忠告、助言
□ already	副もう、すでに	□ keep Ving	熟Ｖし続ける
□ hurt	動痛む	□ anyway	副いずれにせよ
□ beat	動打つ、殴る	□ cool	形かっこいい
□ when	接 .....とき	□ like 〜	前〜のような
□ kid	名子供	□ pick	動入念に選ぶ
□ compared to 〜	熟〜と比較すると		
□ forget	動忘れる forget - forgot - forgotten		

"Kind of. Since my parents abandoned me because they owed someone a lot of money, and I've been alone and homeless for a while, I wanted to lose my family name. I don't have a family anyway. I'm all alone in this world." she said with a charming smile. The crowd froze again.

"Well... Meg... Let's talk about your hobbies. What do you do in your free time?"

"I watch TV and read comic books and magazines. I had collected a lot from garbage piles, but I lost all

WORD LIST

☐ kind of	熟そんなところ	☐ lose	動失う lose - lost - lost
☐ since	接 ..... して以来	☐ talk about ~	熟 ~について話す
☐ abandon	動見捨てる、諦める	☐ free time	熟暇な時
☐ owe	動借りている	☐ comic book	熟マンガ本
☐ a lot of ~	熟たくさんの~	☐ magazine	名雑誌
☐ alone	形たった一人で	☐ collect	動集める
☐ homeless	形家のない	☐ a lot	熟たくさん
☐ for a while	熟しばらくの間	☐ garbage	名生ゴミ、がらくた
☐ want to V	熟 Vしたい	☐ pile	名積み重ね、山

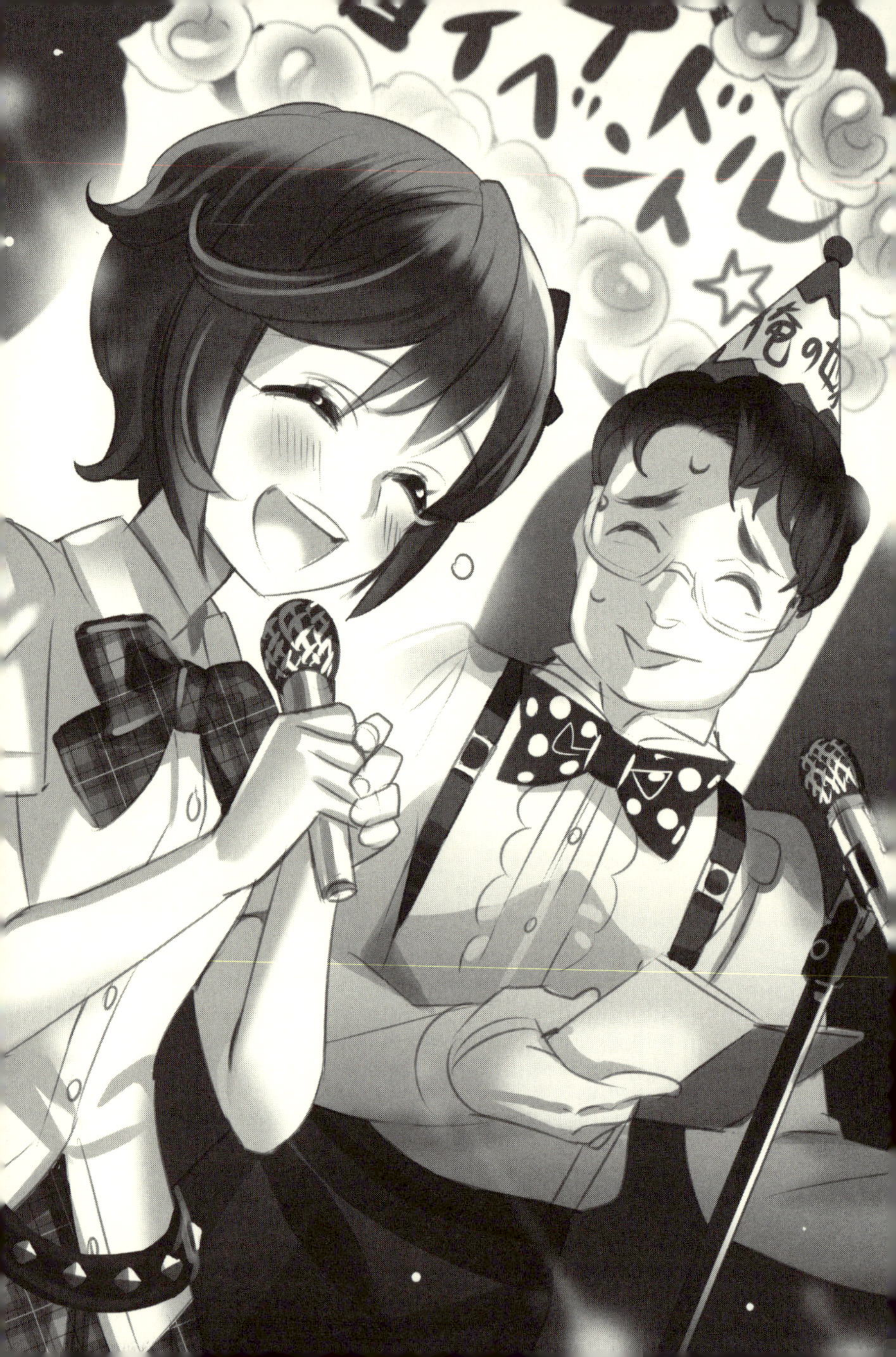
俺の

of them in yesterday's flood. Well, my tent and everything were washed away." She was smiling, and she spoke like she was talking about the last lunch she had. The MC couldn't respond, so she continued.

"I had nowhere to go, so I was in a back alley eating the bread I had bought with a coin I had found at a video arcade. That's when I was attacked by some delinquent boys. One of them held a knife to me. I wished I could die there because I thought I'd be better dead than live a life like that. However, I was saved. It was a miracle. I can't believe I'm here in front of you in fancy clothes like this. I feel like I'm dreaming. Tomorrow, I have to go to the city office and maybe to a home. Well, it can't be helped. I'm homeless after all. I think it's my fate. Some people like me are just born unlucky. I think I need to admit that. I thank God that even for a day I could experience being a pop star. I will never forget meeting you people." She managed to smile through her words.

"Well... Meg... That's... quite..." The MC was at a

WORD LIST

- save 動救う
- miracle 名奇跡
- fancy 形ぜいたくな、装飾的な
- dream 動夢見る
- maybe 副かもしれない
- it can't be helped 熟どうしようもない
- after all 熟結局
- fate 名運命
- be born C 形 C で生まれる
- unlucky 形運が悪い
- need to V 熟 V する必要がある
- admit 動認める
- God 名神
- even 〜 副〜でさえ
- experience 動経験する
- manage to V 熟なんとか V する
- be at a loss for words 熟言葉に詰まる

loss for words. The crowd was silent, too. An awkward silence lasted for several seconds.

Meg thought the boys didn't like her, but anyway she kept smiling. She regretted talking about her misery. She thought it did not fit the occasion. She didn't know what to talk about anymore and began to feel nervous.

Suddenly a boy stood up and yelled, "Meg! Meg!" He was in tears. Then the boys began to stand up one after another, and they also started yelling, "Meg!

WORD LIST

- silent 形静かな
- awkward 形気まずい、不器用な
- silence 名静けさ
- last 動続く
- for several seconds 熟数秒間
- regret 動後悔する
- misery 名惨めさ
- fit 動合う、ふさわしい
- occasion 名時、機会
- anymore 副もはや
- nervous 形緊張して、神経質な
- suddenly 副突然
- stand up 熟立ち上がる
  stand - stood - stood
- yell 動大声をあげる、鋭く叫ぶ
- in tears 熟涙を浮かべて
- one after another 熟次々に

Meg! Meg!" Finally all of them were standing and cheering.

Meg couldn't believe what was happening. She had just talked about her experiences, and now all the people there were supporting her like they were her fans.

The music started, and Meg began singing. She was sometimes off key, but the crowd didn't care. She didn't care, either. They continued cheering, and Meg kept smiling.

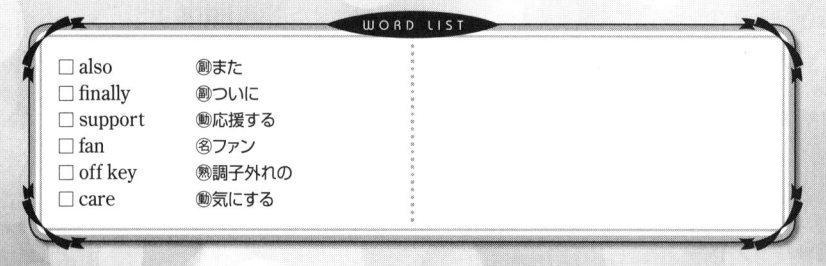

WORD LIST

- also — 副また
- finally — 副ついに
- support — 動応援する
- fan — 名ファン
- off key — 熟調子外れの
- care — 動気にする

In the locker room backstage, Mr. Fuyumoto was smiling, too.

To be continued

WORD LIST

- □ backstage 　 ㊌舞台裏で
- □ smile 　 ㊌微笑む

MEG the Miracle Idol

MEG
the Miracle Idol
Vol. 1
You can be a Star!

Chapter 11

Will You be my Daughter?

Will You be my Daughter?

Mr. Fuyumoto took Meg to a legal office. The lawyer said Meg needed a foster parent, or she would be sent to a home for kids without parents. The lawyer explained the details to Meg, and after that Mr. Fuyumoto said, "Meg, I called the police and the city office. Your parents are officially missing now. There's only one way to keep you out of a home.

"What's that?" Meg asked.

WORD LIST

☐ legal office	熟法律事務所
☐ lawyer	名法律家、弁護士
☐ foster parent	熟里親
☐ explain	動説明する
☐ detail	名詳細
☐ call	動電話をする、呼ぶ
☐ the police	熟警察
☐ city office	熟役所
☐ officially	副正式に
☐ missing	形行方不明の
☐ keep A out of B	熟AをBに入らせない

Chapter 11

"Well, I will adopt you. You will become my daughter. You don't have to call me "Dad" or anything, and you can keep working as a pop star. That's the only way. You can keep it a secret. I'll even give you an apartment to live in."

Meg didn't understand why Mr. Fuyumoto was so kind to her, and she somehow felt it was wrong to accept this generous offer.

"Well... That's very kind of you, but there's no way I can accept such a favor from you. I want to work...

WORD LIST

☐ adopt	動養子にする、採用する	☐ kind	形親切な
☐ daughter	名娘	☐ somehow	副どういうわけか、なぜか
☐ have to V	熟Vしなければならない	☐ feel	動感じる feel - felt - felt
☐ keep Ving	熟Vし続ける	☐ accept	動受け入れる
☐ as ~	前～として	☐ generous	形寛大な
☐ pop star	熟人気歌手	☐ offer	名申し出
☐ keep O C	熟OをCにしておく	☐ there's no way (that)	
☐ secret	名秘密		熟.....ということはあり得ない
☐ apartment	名アパート	☐ favor	名好意

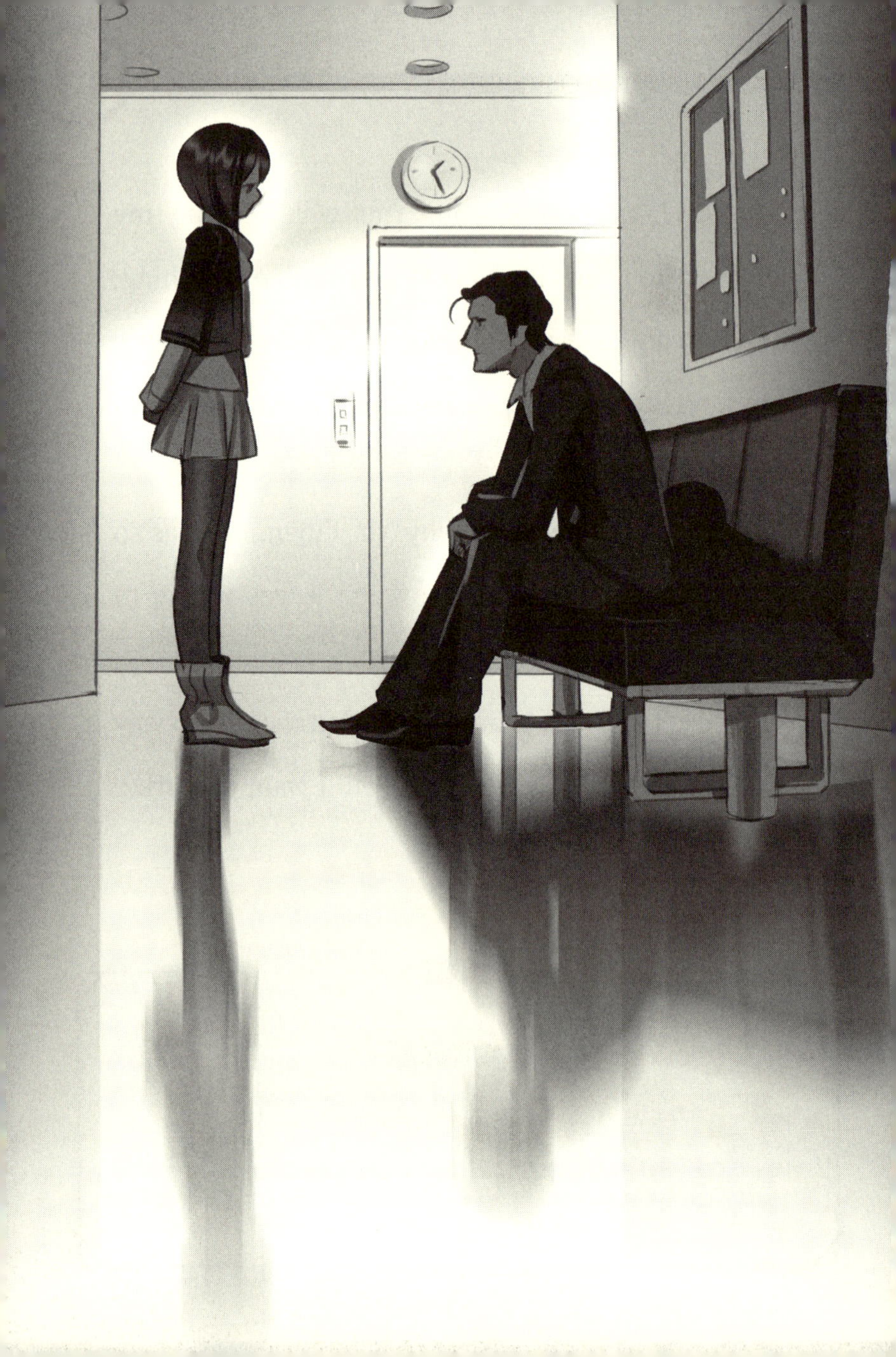

but..."

"You don't have to decide right now. Think about it. You have all day. You should know I think you're very special. The boys' reaction in that idol cafe. That was not something you see every day. You have the power to move people. You are not just a cute teenage pop star. You have the potential to be a super idol."

"I don't think I'm that special."

"Yes, you are. You should know you are a diamond in the rough. I want to refine you into a pure diamond,

---

WORD LIST

☐ decide	動決心する	☐ rough	名原石、荒地
☐ right now	熟すぐに	☐ refine	動磨く、精製する
☐ reaction	名反応	☐ pure	形純粋な、全くの
☐ move	動感動させる		
☐ cute	形可愛い		
☐ potential	名可能性、潜在能力		

a super idol."

"Super idol? Are you serious? I'm just a homeless girl."

"You should have seen yourself in that idol cafe. In such a short time you grabbed everybody's hearts. No other girl could do that."

Meg doubted what Mr. Fuyumoto was saying, but she thought if it was true at all, she would do anything to be an idol.

"This might be the only chance God will give me."

WORD LIST	
☐ serious　形本気の	☐ God　名神
☐ should have Vpp　熟 V すべきだったのに	
☐ grab ~ 's heart　熟~の心を捉える	
☐ doubt　動疑う	
☐ if .....　接もし ..... ならば	
☐ at all　熟仮にも、いやしくも	

She thought to herself.

Later that day, Meg accepted Mr. Fuyumoto's offer.

To be continued

WORD LIST

- think to oneself 熟 (心の中で) 考える
  think - thought - thought
- offer 名 申し出

MEG the Miracle Idol

MEG
the Miracle Idol

Vol. 1

You can be a Star!

Chapter **12**

The First Lesson

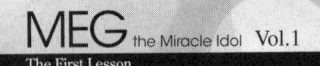

The First Lesson

Although Meg had her first public appearance in Akihabara, it was not her official debut. Mr. Fuyumoto said Meg had to go through several weeks of boot camp at the school he owned before her official debut. She needed to refine her skills.

A lot of young boys and girls who wanted to be actors and pop stars in the future studied there. They came to this school after their regular school on

WORD LIST

☐ although	接 ……だけれども	☐ need to V	熟 Vする必要がある
☐ public	形 公の、公衆の	☐ refine	動 磨く、精製する
☐ appearance	名 出現、出演	☐ skill	名 技術
☐ official	形 正式な	☐ a lot of ~	熟 たくさんの~
☐ debut	名 デビュー	☐ want to V	熟 Vしたい
☐ have to V	熟 Vしなければならない	☐ actor	名 俳優
☐ go through ~	熟 ~を経験する	☐ pop star	熟 人気歌手
☐ boot camp	熟 新人訓練所、新兵訓練基地	☐ in the future	熟 将来は
☐ own	動 所有する	☐ regular	形 通常の

weekdays and also on Saturdays and Sundays. This school was one of the most prestigious in Japan, and a lot of pop stars made their debuts from this school.

Meg started going to a regular school. Every day, after school, and on weekends, she was to attend Mr. Fuyumoto's school and learn singing and dancing.

It was Meg's first day at the school. The first class was a dance class. There were about 20 students there. The instructor was a young woman with a perfect figure. She asked Meg to come up to the

---

WORD LIST

- on weekdays 熟平日に
- also 副また
- prestigious 形一流の
- make a debut 熟デビューする
- every day 熟毎日
- after school 熟放課後
- on weekends 熟週末に
- attend 動通う、出席する
- instructor 名指導者
- figure 名形、プロポーション
- come up to 〜 熟〜に達する

MEG the Miracle Idol Vol.1
The First Lesson

front.

Meg was more nervous than when she had gone on the stage in Akihabara. She was perspiring a little.

"All right, people. I'd like to introduce a new student, Meg. She is going to make her official debut in a few weeks. Meg, say hi to the guys."

"Hi. Nice to meet you all. Since I'm just starting here, I don't know how to dance or how to sing well like you guys. I'd appreciate it if you guys could help me learn," said Meg, but the students were very

---

WORD LIST

- front 名前方
- nervous 形緊張して、神経質な
- when ..... 接 ..... とき
- go on the stage 熟舞台に立つ
- perspire 動汗をかく
- would like to V 熟Vしたい
- introduce 動紹介する
- say hi to ~ 熟~に挨拶をする
- since ..... 接 ..... なので
- how to V 熟Vする方法、Vの仕方
- like ~ 前~のような（に）
- appreciate 動ありがたく思う、正しく理解する

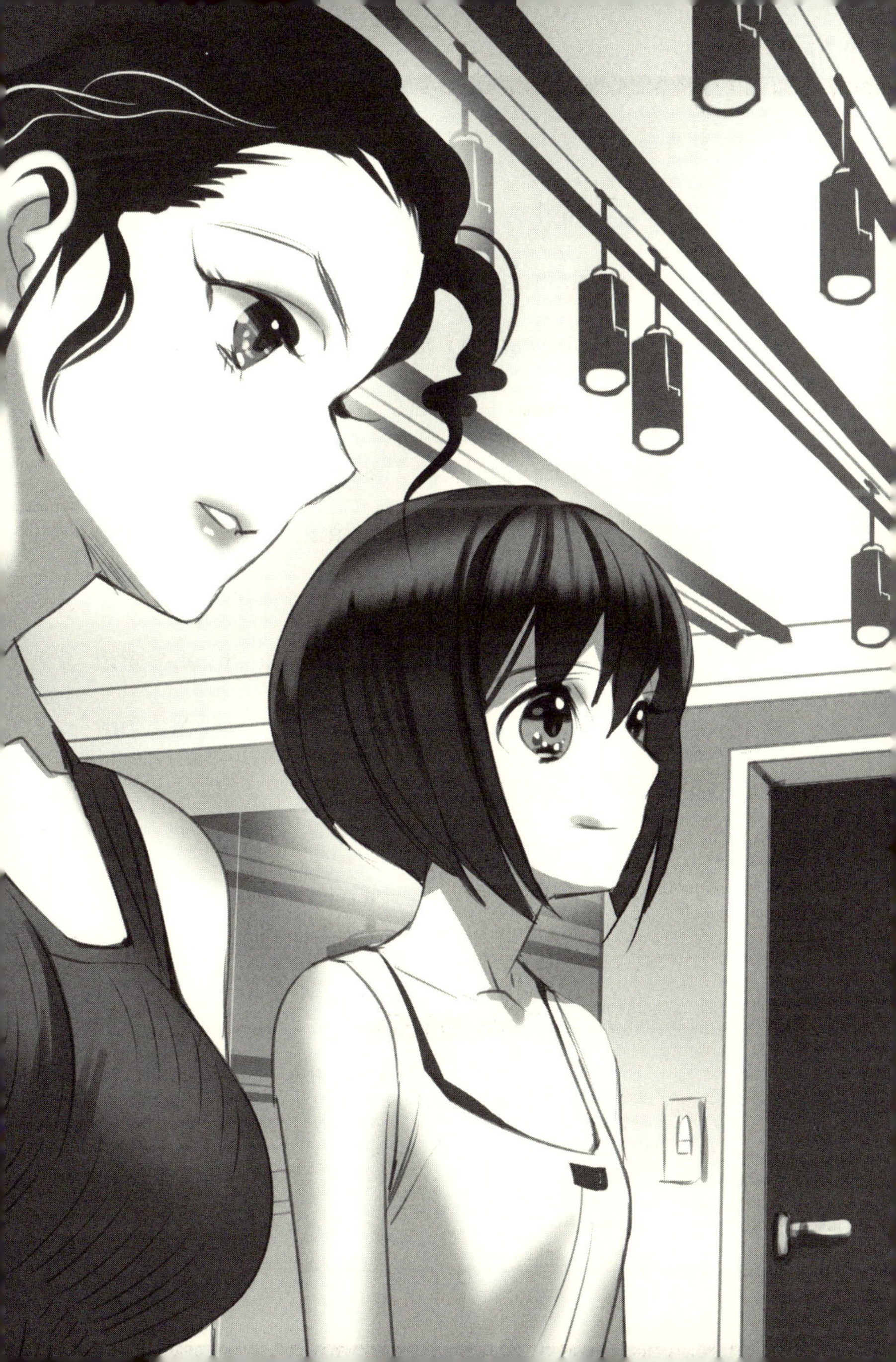

cold. They seemed very jealous.

The lesson started. Meg tried to follow the other students, but she couldn't dance well and made a lot of mistakes.

One girl whispered to her, "I can't believe somebody like you got the position. Did you sleep with Mr. Fuyumoto?"

Meg tried to deny it, but the girl looked away and ignored her. Meg smiled to the other students, but they all avoided eye contact with Meg.

WORD LIST

- cold 形〈人・性格などが〉冷淡な
- seem C 熟 C のように思われる
- jealous 形 嫉妬して
- try to V 熟 V しようと試みる
- follow 動 後について行く
- make a mistake 熟 間違える
  make - made - made
- whisper to ~ 熟 ~にささやく
- deny 動 否定する
- look away 熟 目をそらす
- ignore 動 無視する
- smile 動 微笑む
- avoid 動 避ける
- eye contact 熟 目を合わせること

Chapter 12

After the lesson, Meg went to the locker room to change and opened her locker.

She found a dead bird there.

To be continued

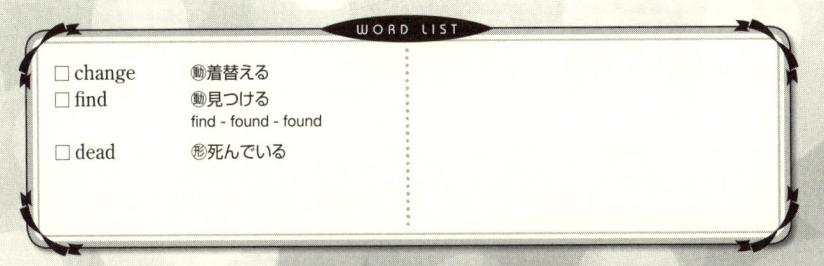

WORD LIST

☐ change	動着替える
☐ find	動見つける
	find - found - found
☐ dead	形死んでいる

MEG the Miracle Idol

MEG
the Miracle Idol

Vol. 1

You can be a Star!

Chapter 13

• • • • • • •

I will be a Star, not You.

I will be a Star, not You.

Naomi Yasuda was born into a very rich family. Her father was the CEO of a very famous cosmetics company, Yasuda. Naomi had attended a ballet school and a music school since she was seven years old. She was now sixteen years old. Her dream was to be a super idol like Momo Sakura.

She was beautiful with big eyes and a straight nose, and she looked very smart. She was 160

WORD LIST

- be born into ~ 熟 ~(の家庭)に生まれる
- CEO 名 chief executive officer の略 最高経営責任者
- cosmetics 名 化粧品
- attend 動 通う、出席する
- ballet 名 バレエ
- since ..... 接 ..... して以来
- dream 名 夢
- like ~ 前 ~のような
- straight 形 まっすぐな
- look C 熟 C に見える
- smart 形 賢い

centimeters tall and was very slim.

She trained very hard to be a good dancer and singer. She spent every Saturday and Sunday at Mr. Fuyumoto's school. In fact, she was the very best in dancing and singing at the school. Everybody had thought she was going to be the next to make a debut, when suddenly it was announced that a girl named Meg would make her debut in a few weeks, and she was going to spend several weeks at the school to prepare for her debut.

WORD LIST

□ slim	形ほっそりとした
□ train	動訓練する
□ spend	動〈時間を〉過ごす spend - spent - spent
□ in fact	熟実際に
□ the very + 最上級	熟本当に、確かに

□ next to ~	熟~に最も近い
□ make a debut	熟デビューする
□ when	接..... とき
□ suddenly	副突然
□ announce	動公表する、知らせる
□ prepare for ~	熟~の準備をする

MEG the Miracle Idol　Vol.1
I will be a Star, not You.

Naomi thought it was very unfair. When she heard about it, she found herself trembling with rage.

"I need to do something about this, but what?" she thought to herself.

The day before Meg's first class, Naomi found a pigeon lying dead on the veranda of her house. She wrapped it in a handkerchief and put it in her bag. When she got to the school, she secretly put the dead bird in Meg's locker.

When Naomi saw Meg for the first time at the

WORD LIST

- unfair　形不公平な
- find O C　熟 O が C だとわかる
- tremble　動震える
- rage　名激怒
- need to V　熟 V する必要がある
- think to oneself　熟（心の中で）考える
  think - thought - thought
- pigeon　名ハト
- lie　動横たわる
  lie - lay - lain - lying
- dead　形死んでいる
- veranda　名ベランダ
- wrap　動包む
- handkerchief　名ハンカチ
- secretly　副秘密に
- for the first time　熟初めて

lesson, she got all the more jealous. Although her dancing was terrible, she felt Meg had something special. She was not only pretty, but she also had some special aura around her, which Naomi wished she had herself.

When Naomi saw that Meg was dancing beside her, she couldn't help whispering to her, "I can't believe somebody like you got the position. Did you sleep with Mr. Fuyumoto?"

She hated herself for saying something like that,

WORD LIST

- all the more ~ 熟 なおいっそう~
- jealous 形 嫉妬して
- although ..... 接 ..... だけれども
- terrible 形 ひどい
- not only A but also B 熟 AだけでなくBも
- aura 名 オーラ
- wish ..... 動 ..... であればいいのだがと思う
- beside ~ 前 ~の隣に（そばで）
- cannot help Ving 熟 Vせざるを得ない
- whisper to ~ 熟 ~にささやく
- like ~ 前 ~のような
- hate oneself for ~ 熟 ~で自己嫌悪に陥る

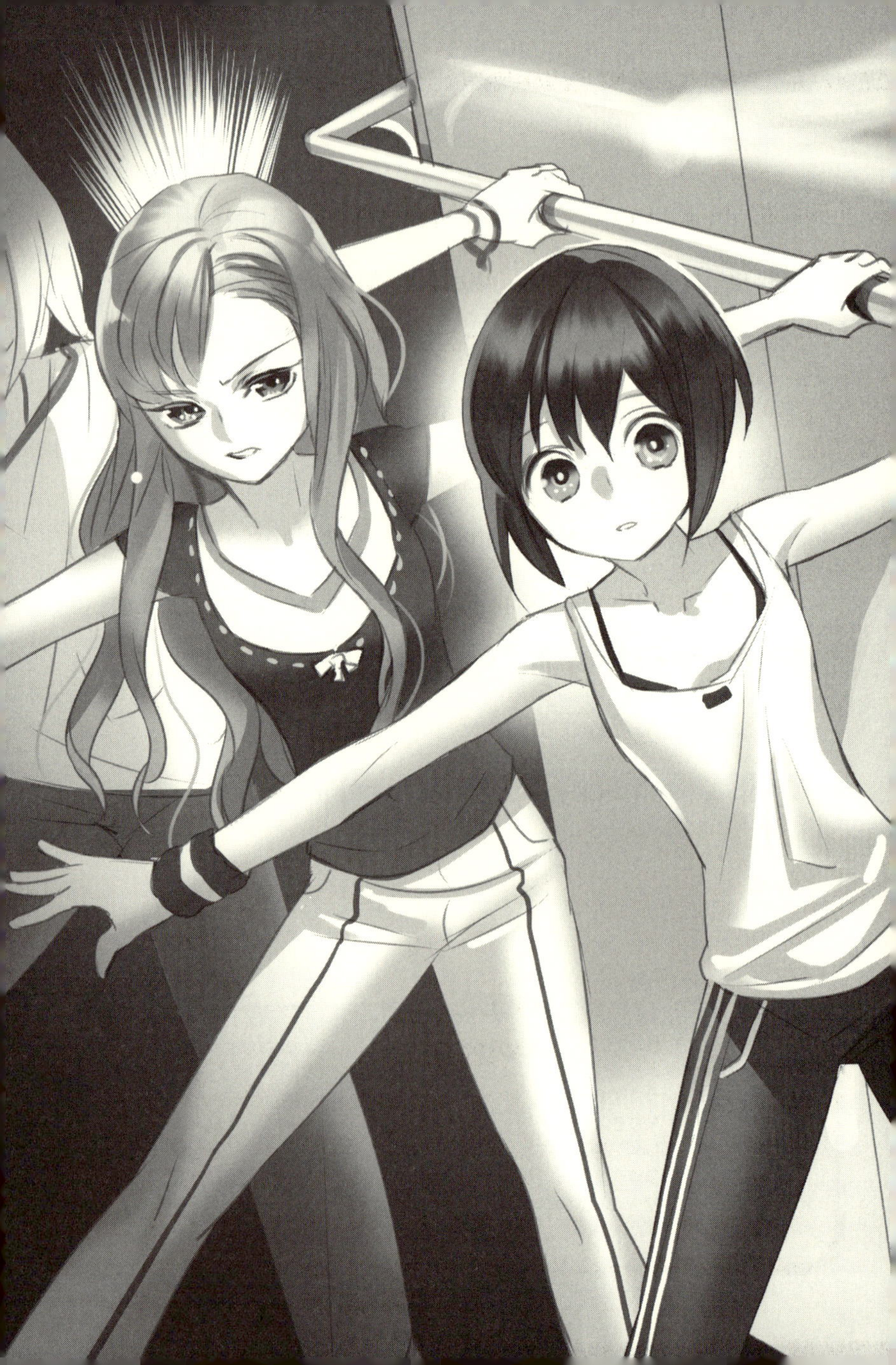

but couldn't help herself.

Naomi was curious about how Meg would react to the dead bird she had put in Meg's locker, and she secretly watched Meg in the locker room.

When Meg found the bird, she didn't yell or do anything. She just wrapped the bird in her handkerchief and put it in her bag.

To be continued

WORD LIST

☐ cannot help oneself	☐ handkerchief ㊜ハンカチ
㊥自分を抑えられない	
☐ curious ㊗好奇心が強い	
☐ react ㊙反応する	
☐ yell ㊙叫ぶ	
☐ wrap ㊙包む	

MEG the Miracle Idol

MEG
the Miracle Idol
Vol. 1
You can be a Star!

Chapter 14

I will Fly High for You.

I will Fly High for You.

Meg was walking along the riverbank looking at the beautiful sunset. The red evening sky was reflected on the surface of the river.

Naomi was secretly following Meg, and she saw Meg stop and sit down off the trail. Meg began to dig in the ground with a wooden stick she had found nearby. When she finished making a small hole, she took out the bird from her bag, and began burying it.

WORD LIST

□ along ~	前〜に沿って	□ dig	動掘る
□ riverbank	名川岸、川の土手	□ ground	名地面
□ look at ~	熟〜を見る	□ wooden	形木製の
□ sunset	名日没、夕焼け	□ stick	名棒きれ
□ reflect	動反射する	□ nearby	副近くで
□ surface	名表面	□ when	接 ..... とき
□ secretly	副秘密に	□ hole	名穴
□ follow	動従う、続く	□ take out ~	熟〜を取り出す
□ trail	名道、跡	□ bury	動埋める

Chapter 14

Then she stood up and went to the river, and found a big round stone. She came back and put the stone on the bird's grave, knelt down, laced her fingers, and said, "I know you wanted to sing more. I know you wanted to fly more. You must have been just like me. I'll sing and fly for you. I will fly high. I will never give up. However tough this world may be, I will never give up on my dreams."

Several meters behind stood Naomi. She overheard Meg's words. Suddenly she yelled, "No,

---

WORD LIST

☐ stand up	熟立ち上がる stand - stood - stood		kneel - knelt - knelt
☐ round	形丸い	☐ lace one's fingers	熟指を組み合わせる
☐ stone	名石	☐ want to V	熟Vしたい
☐ come back	熟戻る come - came - come	☐ fly	動飛ぶ
☐ put	動置く	☐ must have Vpp	熟Vしたに違いない
☐ grave	名墓	☐ give up	熟諦める
☐ kneel down	熟ひざまずく	☐ however	副どんなに ..... とも
		☐ tough	形難しい、丈夫な
		☐ overhear	動ふと耳にする

MEG the Miracle Idol Vol.1
I will Fly High for You.

that's not fair. You can't. It is me that will fly high. I devoted all my life to becoming a star. It's not going to be you. It's going to be me."

Naomi began to cry.

Meg turned around and saw Naomi crying.

"Oh, you... Why...? I don't know what I did to you, but if I offended you in any way, I'm sorry. You might think this is unfair, but this is the only chance I have in my life. I can't lose this," said Meg.

"No. No. I... I..." Naomi began to falter and fell.

―― WORD LIST ――

☐ fair	形公平な	☐ unfair	形不公平な
☐ devote	動捧げる	☐ lose	動失う
☐ cry	動泣く	☐ falter	動ふらつく、ためらう
☐ turn around	熟振り向く	☐ fall	動倒れる、落ちる
☐ if	接もし ..... ならば		fall - fell - fallen
☐ offend	動感情を害する		

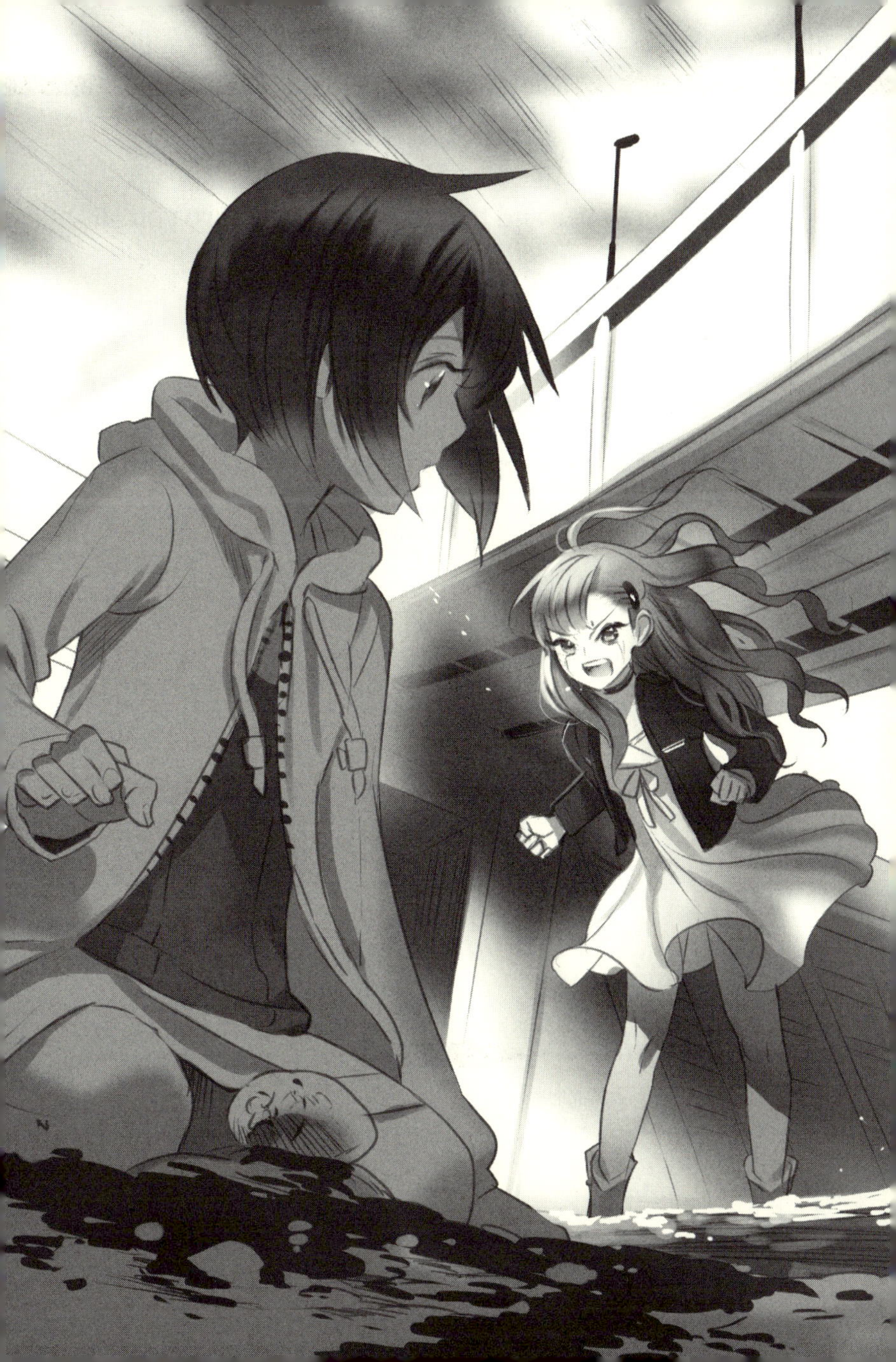

Meg ran to her and talked to her. "Hey. Are you all right? Can you hear me?"

But there was no response.

To be continued

The End of Volume One

WORD LIST

- talk to ～　　熟～に話しかける
- response　　名反応、返答

MEG
the Miracle Idol
Vol. 1
You can be a Star!

和訳

Translation

MEG the Miracle Idol Vol.1

和訳

Chapter 1 Where're Mom and Dad?

親がいない!

鈴木メグは東京の下町に生まれた。彼女の父親は車の小さな部品を作る小さな町工場を経営していた。母親はそこで彼を手伝っていた。工場は小さく、4人の作業員がいたが、彼らの給料を払っていくのも精一杯だった。父と母はいつも忙しく、メグとあまり話すことはなかった。彼らはメグと一緒に食事をすることもほとんどなかった。

メグが小学生の時、彼女の友達はいつも自分たちが行ったテーマパークや映画のことを話していたが、メグは会話に入ることができなかった。日曜日ですら、母親は働いていて、メグをどこかに連れて行く時間もお金もなかった。父親は、休みの日はほとんど家にいることはなかった。彼は、いつも競馬やパチンコや他の賭博場に出かけていた。家にいても、酔っ払って母親を怒鳴りつけているのだった。彼はしばしばメグや母親を殴ることもあった。

友達と違って、メグは可愛い洋服も、立派なオモチャもテレビゲームも持っていなかった。いつも白のTシャツとボロボロのジーンズをはいていた。髪はボサボサで男の子のようだった。彼女は大きくて可愛い目をしていたが、分厚いレンズの安っぽい銀縁メガネがそれを隠してしまっていた。

中学校では、クラスの子供たちが彼女をからかい始めた。だから、彼女は授業をサボり始め、家にいてテレビを見て過ごすようになった。テレビが彼女の唯一の友達だった。彼女はテレビのスクリーンを通して夢のような世界を見ていたのだ。それだけが、惨めな生活からの逃避手段だった。

和訳

　メグはテレビの向こう側の世界に住みたいと思っていた。彼女はとても小さな頃から、アイドルたちのまねをするのが大好きだった。他には何もすることがなかったので、歌うことや踊ることが大好きだった。もう彼女はとても上手に歌ったり踊ったりすることができるようになっていたが、彼女自身は自分がいったい上手なのかどうかは分からなかった。

　彼女の憧れは、桜モモという人気アイドルだった。彼女はとても可愛く、歌が上手かった。まだ16歳なのにいつも面白い話をしていた。その時メグは15歳だった。たった1歳年上の子があんなに上手に歌ったり話したりすることができるなんて信じることができなかった。

　無理だとは分かっていたが、メグはモモのようになりたかった。彼女は、何千回もモモの歌を歌い、モモのように踊る練習をした。彼女はモモのヒット曲のほとんどを覚えた。彼女がモモのように歌ったり踊ったりしている時には、彼女は惨めな生活を忘れることができるのだった。

　ある日、彼女の両親は忙しく家具を片付けていた。あまりにもうるさかったので、メグは出かけることにした。公園に行き、ゴミの山の中から拾ったマンガを読みながら一日を過ごした。

　メグが戻って来た時には、ドアの鍵が開いていた。そして家には誰もいなかった。たくさんの家具がなくなっていた。メグは両親の帰りを待ったが、9時を過ぎても彼らは帰って来なかった。とてもお腹が空いたので、冷蔵庫から豆腐を取り出し、醤油をかけて食べた。

　彼女は両親のことがあまり好きではなかったが、空っぽの家に夜一人でいるのはとても寂しく感じた。彼女は泣きそうな気持ちになった。だから、元気を出すために歌を歌って過ごした。

　11時くらいに、誰かがドアをノックした。メグは両親が戻って来たのだと思いドアを開けた。そこには、ヤクザのような風貌の中年の男が立っていた。

MEG the Miracle Idol Vol.1

和訳

Chapter 2　The House is Gone.

家がなくなっちゃった！

P.16

「親はどこにいるんだ？」見知らぬ男は言った。

メグは少し怖かった。彼の話し方は、テレビドラマに出て来るヤクザのようだった。

「分からないわ。戻って来た時にはいなかったから。」メグは答えた。

「じゃあ、逃げたんだな。」

「逃げたってどういうこと？」

P.17

メグは不安になった。彼女には両親が自分にそんなむごいことをしたなんて信じることはできなかった。彼女はどうして彼らが自分を一緒に連れて行かなかったのか、理解することができなかった。彼女はとても悲しい気持ちになった。

「あのな、お前の親は借金が払えなくて逃げたんだ。だから、家と土地をもらわなくちゃ。」

「ダメよ。そんなの。私は住んでるのよ。」

「それは俺の問題じゃない。俺の問題はお前の親に貸した金を回収す

P.18

ることだ。奴らがいなくなってしまったから、家と土地の権利は俺のものだ。まあ、家は古過ぎるから、明日の朝一番で解体して、土地を売るつもりだ。完全に合法だからな。」

「ダメよ。そうすると、私の行き場がなくなっちゃうわ。」

「それは、俺の問題じゃない。聞こえなかったのか？　完全に合法なんだ。役所でも何でも行くんだな。」

そう言って男はいなくなった。

次の朝、メグが目を覚ますと、彼女は家の外で大きな音を聞いた。彼

女は寝る時にいつも着ていたジャージのまま外に出た。

その日は3月の曇った日で、朝の空気にメグは少し震えた。

二台のブルドーザーが止まっていて、何人かの作業員がいた。彼らの一人が言った。「よし、子供が出たぞ。始めよう。」

そして、ブルドーザーが家に突っ込み解体を始めた。

メグには家がバラバラになっていくのを見ていることしかできなかった。彼女は言葉を発することができなかった。動くこともできなかった。目には涙が込み上げて来た。

誰かが、後ろからメグの肩を叩いた。振り向くとそこには、昨夜出会った男が立っていた。

「人生は残酷だ。その事実を受け入れなきゃな。お前のせいじゃないんだからな。自分を責めるなよ。」

彼は、そう言うとメグに封筒を渡し、いなくなった。

メグは封筒を握りしめ、そこで数分間立ち尽くしていた。彼女の顔は青く、目からは涙が流れ続けた。

そしてメグは封筒を開けた。すると、そこには一万円札がたくさん入っていた。

Chapter 3　Easy Homeless Life

うきうきテント生活

メグはどこに行けばよいのか、分からなかった。彼女は東京の繁華街をふらついていた。彼女の目には涙がたまっていた。彼女が上を見上げた時、建物の壁の大きなテレビが目に入った。スクリーンの中では桜モモが歌っていた。彼女は立ち止まり数分間スクリーンを見ていた。

MEG the Miracle Idol Vol.1

和訳

P25　彼女はつぶやいた。「どうしてこんなに世界は私にむごいことをするの？ モモも私と同じくらいの歳なのに、私は今、ホームレスで、彼女はあのテレビの中の世界。でももうそのことは考えないようにしよう。どうやって生きていくのかを考えなければならないわ。」彼女は涙をぬぐった。

　メグは知らない男からもらった封筒のことを思い出した。メグは封筒から紙幣を取り出してそれを数えてみた。15枚だった。メグにとってそれは大金だったが、どう使ってよいのか見当がつかなかった。

P26　彼女には、役所以外に行く場所がなかったが、彼女は行きたくなかった。もしそこへ行けば、たぶん、規則が厳しい施設に入れられるだろう。彼女は自由を失いたくはなかった。

　メグは自活することに決めた。彼女は店に行きテントと必要なキャンプ用品を買った。また、食料と洋服も買い込んだ。彼女は持っていた半分の金を使ったが、一人で生きていくのに十分な物を手に入れた。

　メグは川辺にテントを立てた。雨を避けるために橋の下に立てた。いったん出来上がると、そこはとても居心地が良かった。近くには銭湯とコインランドリーがあった。彼女が必要なものはすべて揃っていたのだ。

P28　彼女はたくさんのマンガや雑誌をゴミの山から集めた。そして、バーゲンでポータブルテレビを買った。彼女は全く退屈することはなかった。毎日彼女は川辺で歌ったり踊ったり、テントの中でテレビを見たりマンガを読んだりして過ごした。

　メグはそんな風にして数週間を過ごしたが、ついにはお金が不足してきた。

P29　そこで、彼女は自動販売機やゲームセンターで人々が取り忘れた小銭を集め始めた。驚いたことに、銭湯とコインランドリーの分は集めることができた。食べ物に関しては近所の店からパンやフルーツを万引きし

ていた。彼女にはそれが悪いことだとは分かっていた。彼女は罪悪感を感じていたが、どうしようもなかった。彼女はこの自由を失いたくはなかったのだ。だから、彼女は捕まらないように細心の注意を払っていた。

メグはこの生活が気に入っていた。彼女をいじめたり殴ったりする人は誰もいなかった。そして好きなだけ歌ったり踊ったりすることができた。彼女はずっとこんな風に生活したいと思った。

Chapter 4　Unhappy Birthday

アンハッピーバースデー

何ヶ月かが過ぎ、もう9月になった。台風の季節がやって来て、大きな台風が東京地区を襲った。次の日の朝、川は溢れていた。水はテントのところまで上がって来た。彼女はテントから逃げなければならなかった。彼女にはテントから物を持ち出す時間はなかった。何とか持ち出すことができたのは、メガネだけだった。彼女はジャージを着ていた。

彼女は水がテントと彼女の財産すべてを飲み込むのを見守った。家がなくなるのを見たのは二度目だった。まるで映画を見ているようだった。今度は涙は出て来なかった。悲しいことにこの日は彼女の16歳の誕生日だった。メグは「人生はとても残酷だ。」という知らない男が言った言葉を思い出した。メグはこの言葉は本当だと思った。少なくとも彼女にとっては…

彼女は午後はずっとゲームセンターでコインを集めていた。たった100円しか見つけることができず、それでは、やっとパンがひとつ買えるだけだった。

夕方には、メグは裏路地に座ってパンを食べていたが、彼女は自暴自

MEG the Miracle Idol Vol.1

和訳

棄になっていた。もう次の朝には役所に行くしかないと思った。彼女は自由を失うことをとても悲しく思った。

　突然三人の酔っ払った少年が彼女を囲んだ。彼らは髪を染め、刺青をしていて、とても危険に見えた。

　「お嬢さんこんなところで何してるのかなあ？　一緒に来ない？　いろんなこと教えてあげるよ。へへ。」一人の少年が言った。

P.36

　「ほっといて…でなきゃ、殺して。」メグは言った。

　「いいよ。でも後でね。」

　そう言って、少年は彼女の腕をつかんだ。

　「やめて。」メグは叫び、逃げようとした。でももう一人の少年が反対の腕をつかんだ。

　彼女は叫び続けていたが、誰も来てはくれなかった。彼女の目からは涙が流れた。

Chapter 5　Is He a Hero or...?

白馬の騎士？

P.38

　メグは叫び続けていた。そうすると、三番目の男がナイフを取り出して言った。「静かにしろ。そうしないとけがをするぞ。」

　突然、ダークグレーのスーツを着た男が路地へと走り込んで来た。彼の服装はとてもオシャレで映画スターのようだった。とても若い男たちを相手にできるようではなかった。彼はビシッと整ったヘアスタイルで、30代くらいに見えた。

P.39

　メグは少しほっとしたが、男を見てとても不安になった。彼女は男が少年たちに袋叩きにされるのではないかと心配した。状況が悪化するか

もしれないと思った。

　少年たちは彼を見て言った。「ほら、けがしたくないんなら、かまうなよ。きれいなスーツに血が付くぞ。あっち行けよ。」

　男は答えた。「違うよ。違うんだ。君たちとけんかをしたいわけじゃない。取引をしたいだけだ。」

　彼は携帯電話を掲げて言った。「その子に金を払おう。その子を放っておいてくれれば、10万円を払おう。それでどうだ？　うちの連中は大通りに止まった車で待ってる。このボタンを押せば飛んでくる。変なことは考えるな。」

　彼には説得力があり、大物であるように見えた。少年たちは彼の言葉に聞き入っていた。それに加え、彼らにとって、10万円は魅力的に響いた。

　「金を先に見せろ。」少年の一人が言った。

　男は財布を取り出し、少年たちの方にそれを投げ、言った。「全部やるよ。全部な。」

　一人の少年がそれを拾い、開けて、言った。「わあ、10万円以上入ってる！　20万くらい入ってる！」

　別の少年がメグに言った。「お前、ラッキーだな。あのおっさんには行儀良くするんだぞ。へへヘッ。」

　メグはほっと息をついて、男に感謝した。しかし、彼女を助けることで男がたくさんお金をなくしたことを申し訳なく思った。

　少年たちがいなくなった後、男はメグに言った。「両親をもうこれ以上心配させるな。お前は家に帰れ。」

　「助けてくれてありがとう。でも私には家がないのよ。どこにも行くところがないの。」メグは泣きながら言った。「何もかもなくしたの。両親も、家も、お金も。どうしていいか分からないわ。」

MEG the Miracle Idol Vol.1
和訳

「分かった。じゃあ、何か飲み物をあげるから、落ち着いてくれ、それから、次に何をするか考えよう。さあ行くぞ。」

メグは男について行き、大通りに大きな黒いレクサスが止めてあるのを見た。

車には誰も乗っていなかった。

Chapter 6 Won't You be an Idol?

アイドルやってみない?

メグと男は車に乗り込んだ。男は運転席に、メグは彼の隣の助手席に座った。

彼女は言った。「仲間はどこにいるの? ハッタリだったのね。」

「もちろんさ。奴らには分かりっこなかった。」

彼は、エンジンをかけた。

「どこに行くの? あなたは誰?」メグは尋ねた。

「うん、私は会社を経営している。私のオフィスに連れて行こう。今夜はそこに泊まればいい。」

「えっ? またハッタリ?」

「違う。本当だ。六本木に行く。そこに会社はある。よかったら、お茶を飲みなさい。」

メグはこの男を信用するのは危険だと思ったが、道で寝るよりはましだと考えた。それに、彼は彼女には悪い人間には思えなかった。彼女は彼のことが何だか気に入っていた。

彼は、メグに缶入りの緑茶を渡し、運転を始めた。メグは缶を開け、お茶を飲んだ。これまでのすべての疲れが込み上げ、眠くなって来た。

「疲れているだろう。少し眠りなさい、着くまでには30分ほどかかるから。」

メグは目を閉じて眠った。

彼女が目を開いた時、目の前には巨大で美しい超高層ビルがそびえていた。彼らは東京でも、最も高級な地区のひとつである、六本木ヒルズにいたのだった。車は建物の地下へと入って行った。

メグは、男は本当に会社のオーナーなのだと思った。

車を停めた後、彼らはエレベーターに乗って32階まで行った。エレベーターのすぐ外には「東京プロダクション」という看板のある受付デスクがあった。デスクの後ろには二人の受付担当が座っていて、彼らの頭上には大きなデジタルディスプレイがあった。その画面には、桜モモを含む多くの有名なテレビタレントの写真が映し出されていた。ここはタレントプロダクションだったのだ。スクリーンに映し出された様々な顔から考えて、メグは有名なプロダクションに違いないと思った。

受付は男に頭を下げて言った。「冬本様、お帰りなさい。」

彼らは部屋に入りソファーに座った。

「あなたは誰なの？」メグは尋ねた。

「会社を所有しているって言っただろう。この芸能プロのオーナーだ。」

「じゃあ、あなたが桜モモやあのスターを全部プロデュースしてるの？」

メグの心臓の鼓動は速くなった。彼女は長い間夢に見ていた世界にとても近いところにいると知って興奮していたのだ。ついに何か良いことが彼女の人生に起こったのだと感じた。

「そうだ。でも、君とは関係のない話だ。今夜はここに泊まってもいいが、明日の朝、役所に連れて行くからな。おっ、ちょっとメガネを取ってごらん。」

冬本の顔はとても真剣だった。彼は熱心にメグのことを見ていた。

MEG the Miracle Idol Vol.1

和訳

P.53

「どうして？」

「いいから。で、立ってごらん。」

「どうして？」

「いいから、言う通りにしなさい。」

メグは立ち上がった。冬本はメグをまじまじと見た。彼はしばらく考えてからメグに言った。「おい、遊びで一日だけアイドルをやってみないか？　ひどい一日だっただろう？　埋め合わせをしてやりたいんだ。どうだ、やってみるか？　本物のアイドルになるわけじゃない。ただの体験だよ。」

Chapter 7　The Transformation

大変身

P.56

メグはドアがノックされる音を聞いて目を覚ました。彼女はまだ前の日に着ていたジャージのままだった。彼女の髪はいつものようにボサボサだった。彼女は自分がどこにいるのかと不思議に思ったが、冬本の会社の一室にいることを思い出した。彼女は毛布からはい出し言った。「はーい。ちょっと待って。」

彼女は前の日に冬本が言ったことを思い出した。彼女は一日アイドルになるのだった。彼女の心臓の鼓動は速くなった。彼女はとても緊張していたが、同時に、桜モモや他のトップスターたちと同じ世界にいるのだと考えて、とても興奮していた。

P.57

彼女がメガネを身に付けて、ドアを開けると、若い女性がそこに立っていた。彼女はとてもオシャレだった。彼女はメグに言った。「私はスタイリストです。冬本さんに、今日のイベントのための準備をするよう

に言われています。一緒に来てください。」まだ、朝の7時だった。

　メグは彼女について行った。そして彼らは、やはり六本木ヒルズにある、ホテルの部屋へとやって来た。メグはシャワーを浴びるように言われ、彼女のために準備された服に着替えた。洋服はぎゅうぎゅうで着心地が悪かったが、とてもオシャレだった。

　その服は学校の制服みたいだったが、オレンジのピンストライプや金属の飾りが付いていた。スカートは少し短かった。ドレスの腰回りはボディラインを強調するためにとてもきつかった。

　そして、メグは美容室へと連れて来られたが、そこにはハンサムなヘアスタイリストがいた。彼は、冬本から、メグの髪をカットし、染めて、スタイリングするように言われていると告げた。それが終わると、もう10時になっていた。彼女は鏡の中の自分を見たが、メガネがないので、はっきりとは見えなかった。メグはポケットからメガネを取り出して身に付けると、かつてのホームレスの少女とは全く違う自分を見てびっくりした。彼女の髪は茶色に染められていて、大きなカールがあった。彼女は六本木ヒルズにいる、金持ちでファッショナブルなティーンエイジの女の子のようだったのだ。

　彼女はまた、ホテルの部屋へと連れて行かれたが、そこにはメイクアップ師がいた。彼の見た目は男だったが、女の子のような話し方だった。メグは彼は男性を好むタイプなのだろうと思った。

　メグは、こんなにも長い時間、彼女のために人がメイクをしてくれることを不思議に感じた。彼女がこんなにも良く扱ってもらったことは今までになかったからだ。彼女は自分にはそんな価値はないと思ったので、少しこの男性に申し訳ないと感じた。

　30分経って、彼はメイキャップを終えた。もうメグは前の彼女とは別人だった。メガネをかけて鏡の中の自分を見た時、彼女は仰天した。

MEG the Miracle Idol Vol.1

和訳

彼女は本物のアイドルのようだったのだ。メグは、スーパーアイドル、桜モモと同じくらい可愛かった。彼女はバラエティー番組に出ている典型的なタレントの少女たちよりも、はるかに美しかった。彼女の外見は特別だった。

冬本が部屋に入って来た。そして彼女を見て、声を上げた。「おお。やっぱりだ。見ろ。すごいぞ。ダイヤモンドの発見だ！」

Chapter 8　Can You Sing a Song?

歌ってみる？

メグは冬本の言葉を信じることができなかった。

「えっ、私がダイヤモンド？」

彼女はとても嬉しかった。彼女のことを誰かが褒めてくれたり、彼女の存在を認めてくれたのは初めてだったのだ。このことは彼女に自信を与え、彼女の目はさらに輝き、彼女の類い希なる美しさを増幅した。

「君の名前は？」冬本はメグに尋ねた。

「メグよ。鈴木メグ。」

「そうか…『メグ』はいいけどな。鈴木は取った方がいいな。」

「何の話？」

「君の芸名だよ。『鈴木』はありきたり過ぎる。だから、ただ『メグ』だけにするのがいいだろうね。」

「いいわ。どちらにしろ、名字はあまり好きじゃないの。それに、もう家族なんていないわけだから。ただメグとだけ呼んで欲しいわ。」

「分かった。じゃあ、君の芸名は『メグ』だ。決まり。で、君は歌は上手いのか？」

「分からないわ。でも桜モモの歌はほとんど歌えるわ。いつもそればかり歌ってたから、歌詞も全部覚えてる。彼女の振り付けもできるわ。どうして？」

「うん、今日は歌わなければならないかもしれない。」

メグはそれを聞いてぎょっとした。

「えっ、今日？　歌うの？　人前で？　ダメ！　無理よ。そんなに上手くないんだから。私の歌なんて、完全に普通なんだから。」

「大丈夫だよ。普通がいいんだ。みんな普通の歌手が好きなんだ。『幸せの涙』歌えるか？」

『幸せの涙』は60年代の古い曲だったが、桜モモをはじめとする多くの歌手がカバーしていた。それは、シンプルなメロディーの典型的なポップソングだった。桜モモの曲としては、それほどのヒットではなかった。

「うん、歌える…でも…」メグは緊張していた。

「歌いなさい。」

「ここで？」

「そうだ。今すぐ。」

メグはメガネを外した。そうすると何もかもがぼやけて見え、もうそれほど緊張しなくなった。彼女は歌い始めた。彼女の歌はそれほどすばらしいというわけでもなかったが、人前で歌うには十分なレベルだった。冬本は感心した。

「うん。君はアイドルに向いている。行くぞ。」冬本は言った。

「どこに？」メグは尋ねた。

「君の一日デビューにぴったりの場所に連れて行ってやる。秋葉原だ。」

MEG the Miracle Idol Vol.1
和訳

Chapter 9　Akihabara

アキバ

P.72

メグと冬本は六本木ヒルズの写真スタジオに行った。メグはそこで1時間ほど、プロの写真家に写真を撮ってもらった。彼は、普通の中年のおじさんに見えたが、とても面白い人だった。彼はメグにポーズの取り方を教えてくれた。彼は、メグがリラックスできるように、写真を撮りながら、ずっとメグに話しかけてくれた。メグは彼のことが気に入った。こんな父親がいてくれるといいなあと思った。

P.73

そして、メグと冬本は駐車場へ行き、大きな黒いレクサスに乗り込んだ。紺色のスーツを着た女性と運転手がすでに車の中にいた。女性は忙しそうに電話をしていた。彼女は膝の上にパソコンを置いていた。メグは、会話の中で彼女が何度も「メグ」という名前を口にしているのを聞いた。メグと冬本が後部座席に座ると、車は走り出した。

およそ30分で彼らは秋葉原に着いた。午後4時になっていた。晴れていたが、9月にしてはそれほど暑くはない日だった。

P.74

秋葉原は時々アニメやアイドルのメッカと呼ばれる。アニメやアイドルが大好きな少年たちが、アニメ関係の品物や好きなアーティストのアルバム、アイドルの写真集を買うために集まるからだ。彼らはまた、メイドカフェを訪れる。そこでは、メイドの衣装をまとった若い少女たちが飲み物を出し、客と歓談する。将来アイドルになりたいと願うたくさんの少女がメイドカフェで働いている。

土曜日だった。メグは車の窓越しに通りが少年たちでごった返しているのを見た。

P.76

冬本は女性に言った。「さあ、酒井さん。彼女にコートとマスクを渡

して。」

彼女はグレーのコートと白いマスクをメグに渡した。

「それを着て、メガネを取らないようにしなさい。」冬本はメグに言った。

メグはそれらを身に付けた。そして女性は車から降りて、メグのためにドアを開けた。メグは混雑した通りに出た。

彼らはおよそ百メートル歩き、四階建てのビルの裏口にたどり着いた。女性がドアを開けると、メグには大きな音楽と歓声が聞こえた。彼らはビルの中の小さなロッカールームに入った。

冬本はメグに言った。「ここは僕が経営するアイドルカフェだ。君はここで1日デビューする。コートとマスクとメガネを取りなさい。この女性が今日の君のマネージャー、酒井さんだ。分からないことがあったら、彼女に聞きなさい。」

「あなたは5時にステージに上がるのよ。5分間司会者と話して一曲歌うの。そして、また5分間司会者と話すのよ。それであなたの出番はおしまい。分かった？」

「うん。でも何を話すの？」メグは心配していた。

「趣味やら何やらね。心配しないで。とにかく常に微笑んで。分かった？微笑むのよ。」

メグは緊張していたが、酒井はとても事務的で、信頼できる話し振りだったのでメグはリラックスできた。

5時になった。司会者は大きなカフェに座っているおよそ百人くらいの客に向かって言った。「さあ、新しいスター、メグを紹介しましょう。」

「さあ、行くのよ。」酒井はそう言って、メグを押し出した。そしてメグはステージに上がった。群衆は喝采を浴びせた。

MEG the Miracle Idol Vol.1

和訳

Chapter 10　Just Keep Smiling!

笑ってればいいから!

P.82

　メグはメガネをしていなかったし、明かりがとてもまぶしかったので、聴衆がよく見えなかった。しかし、100人以上の人々が彼女のために喝采しているのは分かった。

　彼女は司会者の方に走って行ったが、ステージの上のマイクのコードに引っかかって転んだ。そして顔をステージに真っ正面から打ち付けた。群衆は一瞬凍り付いた。しかし、メグが立ち上がると、再び喝采した。

P.83

　メグはこんな間抜けな登場の仕方をしたことにドギマギしたが、気を引きしめて不安を顔に出さないようにした。

　「メグ、大丈夫?」司会者は尋ねた。

　「大丈夫よ。聞いてくれてありがとう。」彼女は微笑みながら答えたが、鼻からは少し血が出ていた。

　「ほんと大丈夫?　鼻血が出ているよ。続けられる?」

　「あら、本当?」彼女はハンカチを取り出して、血を拭き取り、微笑みながら言った。「大丈夫。大丈夫。続けましょう。」

P.84

　「わあ、メグ。もう完全にプロだねえ。痛くないの?」

　「うん、大丈夫よ。子供の頃、私やお母さんはいつもお父さんに殴られてたから。それに比べるとこんなのへっちゃらよ。」彼女は話をする時微笑むという酒井のアドバイスを決して忘れはしなかった。

　「分かった…じゃあとにかく、メグ。君の名前はただ『メグ』だよね。名前だけだよね。かっこいいと思うよ。まるで球界のスター、『ジロー』みたいだよ。自分で芸名選んだの?」

P.85

　「そんな感じかな。親はたくさん借金してたから、私、捨てられちゃ

ったの。で、私しばらくの間、一人でホームレスやってたのね。だから、苗字なんていらないって思ったの。どうせ、家族いないし…私はこの世の中に一人きり。」彼女は可愛く微笑みながら言った。また、聴衆は凍り付いた。

「えっと…メグ、じゃあ趣味について話そうか…暇な時は何してる?」

「テレビを見たりマンガや雑誌を読んだりしてるわ。ゴミの中から、たくさんマンガ集めてたのよ。でも、昨日の台風で全部流されちゃった。そう、テントとか全部流されちゃったのよ。」彼女は微笑んでいた。そして、食べたばかりのランチの話をするような話し振りだった。司会者は反応することができなかったので、彼女は続けた。

「私には行くところがなくなったの。で、ゲームセンターで見つけたコインで買ったパンを裏路地で食べてたの。その時に不良少年に襲われたの。一人は私にナイフを突きつけたわ。あんな生活をしてるくらいなら死んだ方がましだと思ってたから、そこで死にたいと願ったわ。でも、助けられたの。奇跡よ。こんなところでこんなにきれいな洋服を着て、ここでみんなの前にいるなんて信じられないわ。夢のよう。明日は、役所に行って施設に入らなきゃいけないかもしれない。でも、仕方ないわ。結局、私はホームレスだから。私の運命ね。私みたいな人は生まれながらにして不幸なのよ。それを認めなくちゃいけないと思う。1日だけでもアイドルの経験ができたことを神様に感謝するわ。みんなに出会えたことを絶対に忘れない。」彼女は話しながら、何とか微笑み続けた。

「えー、メグ、それは、な、なかなか…」司会者は言葉に詰まった。聴衆もまた音を失った。気まずい沈黙が数秒間続いた。

メグは少年たちが彼女のことを気に入ってくれなかったのかと思ったが、とにかく微笑み続けた。彼女は自分の惨めな暮らしについて話したことを後悔した。場の空気に合わなかったと思ったのだ。彼女はもう何

を話せば良いのか分からなくなり、緊張し始めた。

　突然、一人の少年が立ち上がって叫んだ。「メグ！　メグ！」彼は涙を流していた。そして少年たちは一人ずつ立ち上がり始めた。そしてみんな、叫び始めた。「メグ！　メグ！　メグ！」ついには、全員が立ち上がり喝采を与えていた。

　メグは、起こっている出来事が信じられなかった。ただ自分の経験を話しただけなのに、もう、まるでみんな彼女のファンになったように応援してくれていたのだ。

　音楽が始まり、メグは歌い始めた。彼女の歌は時々音程が外れたが、でも聴衆は気にすることはなかった。彼女も気にしなかった。彼らは喝采を続け、メグは微笑み続けた。

　裏方のロッカールームでは、冬本も微笑んでいた。

Chapter 11　Will You be my Daughter?

娘になる？

　冬本はメグを法律事務所に連れて行った。弁護士はメグには里親が必要だと言った。そうしないと彼女は児童養護施設に入れられることになるのだった。弁護士はメグに詳細を説明した。そしてその後に冬本は言った。

　「メグ、僕は警察と役所に連絡をしてみた。君の両親は現在正式に行方不明ということになっている。君を施設に入れない方法はひとつしかない。」

　「それは何？」メグは尋ねた。

　「そうだね。僕が君を養子にする。君が僕の娘になるわけだ。別に『お

父さん』と呼ばなくちゃいけないとかいうことじゃないけれど、そうすればタレントとして仕事を続けることができる。それしか方法がないんだ。秘密にしててかまわない。住むためのアパートも準備するよ。」

メグはどうして冬本が彼女にそんなに親切なのか理解できなかった。そして、彼女はこの寛大な申し出を受け入れることは何だか間違ったことのように思えた。

「ええ、本当にありがたいんだけれど、そんな好意を受け入れる理由なんて私にはないわ。仕事はしたいけれど…でも…」

「今決める必要はない。考えなさい。一日中考えればいい。君は特別な才能を持っていると僕は考えているんだ。あのアイドルカフェでの男の子たちの反応を見たかい？ あんなことは滅多にない。君には、人を感動させる力がある。君は単なる可愛い10代のタレントじゃないよ。君にはスーパーアイドルになる力があるんだ。」

「私、そんなに特別じゃないわ。」

「いや、特別だよ。君はまだダイヤモンドの原石だ。僕は君を磨き上げてダイヤモンドの宝石を作りたい。スーパーアイドルだ。」

「スーパーアイドル？ 本気なの？ 私はただのホームレスの子よ。」

「アイドルカフェでの君自身の姿を見るべきだったよ。あんな短い時間でみんなの心をつかんだんだ。あんなことができる子は他にいない。」

メグは冬本が言っていることを疑ったが、もしもそれが本当だったら、アイドルになるために何だってやりたいと思った。

「神様がくれたたったひとつのチャンスかもしれないわ。」彼女は考えた。

その後、メグは冬本の申し出を受け入れた。

MEG the Miracle Idol Vol.1

和訳

Chapter 12　The First Lesson

ファーストレッスン

P.102　メグは秋葉原で初めて人前に出たが、それは正式なデビューというわけではなかった。冬本は、メグは、正式にデビューする前に、冬本が経営する学校で、数週間の訓練を受けなければならないと言った。彼女は技術を磨く必要があったのだ。

将来、俳優やタレントになりたい多くの少年少女が、そこで勉強していた。彼らは平日、通常の学校が終わった後や、土曜日や日曜日にこの学校に通った。この学校は、日本で最も権威がある場所のひとつで、多くのアイドルたちがこの学校からデビューしていた。

P.103

メグは通常の学校に通い始めた。毎日、放課後、そして週末は彼女は冬本の学校に通い、歌と踊りを学ぶこととなった。

その学校でのメグの最初の日がやって来た。最初はダンスの授業だった。約20人の生徒たちがいた。インストラクターは完璧な体型をした若い女性だった。彼女は、メグに前に出るように言った。

P.104　メグは秋葉原のステージに立った時よりも緊張していた。少し汗をかいていた。

「はい、みんな。新しい生徒を紹介するわね。メグよ。彼女は数週間後に正式にデビューする予定なの。メグ、みんなに挨拶して。」

「こんにちは。初めまして。まだ始めたばかりなので、踊り方も歌い方も分かりません。みんなに教えてもらえるとありがたいです。」メグはそう言ったが、生徒たちは冷淡だった。彼らは嫉妬しているようだった。

P.106　レッスンが始まった。メグは他の生徒と同じようにしようとしたが、

144

上手く踊ることができず、たくさん間違いをした。

　一人の少女が彼女にささやいた。「あんたみたいな子がデビューするなんて信じられないわ。冬本さんと関係したの？」

　メグはそのことを否定しようとしたが、その子はそっぽを向いて彼女を無視した。メグは他の生徒たちに微笑みかけたが、彼らはみんなメグと目を合わせようとしなかった。

　レッスンの後、メグは着替えるためにロッカー室に行き、彼女のロッカーを開けた。そこには鳥の死骸があった。

Chapter 13　I will be a Star, not You.

スターは私よ！

　安田ナオミは裕福な家庭に生まれた。彼女の父親はとても有名な化粧品会社、ヤスダのCEOであった。ナオミは7歳の頃から、バレエ学校と音楽学校に通っていた。彼女は16歳になっていた。彼女の夢は、桜モモのような、スーパーアイドルになることだった。

　彼女は大きな目とすらりとした鼻をしており、とても賢そうに見えた。彼女の身長は160センチで、とてもスリムだった。

　彼女は踊りや歌が上手になるために懸命に訓練を受けた。毎週土曜日も日曜日も冬本の学校に通って過ごした。実際、歌も踊りも彼女が学校でトップだった。誰もが次にデビューするのは彼女だと思っていたが、そんな時、メグという名前の少女が数週間でデビューするので、学校でデビューの準備のために数週間勉強するのだということが告知された。

　ナオミはそのことをとても不公平だと感じた。それを聞いた時、彼女は怒りに震えていた。

MEG the Miracle Idol　Vol.1

和訳

「何とかしなきゃ。でも何？」彼女は考えた。

メグが初めて授業に参加する前の日、ナオミは彼女の家のベランダにハトの死骸が横たわっているのを見つけた。彼女はそれをハンカチに包んで、カバンの中に入れた。学校に着いた時、彼女は、密かに鳥の死骸をメグのロッカーに入れた。

ナオミが授業で始めてメグを見た時、彼女の嫉妬心はますます強くなった。彼女のダンスはひどいものだったが、メグには何か特別なものがあると感じたのだ。彼女はただ可愛いだけでなく、なにか特別なオーラをまとっていた。そんなオーラをナオミは自分自身も持ちたいと思っていたのだ。

メグがナオミの隣で踊っている時、彼女はこうささやかずにはいられなかった。「あんたみたいな子がデビューするなんて信じられないわ。冬本さんと関係したの？」

彼女はそんなことを言う自分に嫌悪感を持ったが、自分自身を抑えることができなかったのだ。ナオミはメグがロッカーに入れた鳥の死骸を見てどう反応するのか興味があった。そして、ロッカー室でメグのことをのぞき見た。

メグが鳥の死骸を見つけた時、彼女は叫びも何もしなかった。彼女はただ鳥の死骸をハンカチに包み、カバンの中に入れた。

Chapter **14**　I will Fly High for You.

私は飛ぶ!

メグは、美しい夕日を見ながら、川の土手の上を歩いていた。赤い夕日が川面に反射していた。

ナオミは密かにメグの後をつけていた。そして、メグが道からそれたところでしゃがむのを見た。メグは近くで見つけた木の棒で地面を掘り始めた。小さな穴を作り終えた時、彼女は鳥をカバンから取り出し、埋め始めた。

それから彼女は立ち上がって川の方へと歩いて行った。そして大きな丸い石を見つけた。彼女は戻って来て、その石を鳥の墓の上に置き、ひざまずき、指を組んで言った。「もっと歌いたかったでしょう。もっと飛びたかったでしょう。私と同じだったのね。私があなたのために歌い飛ぶわ。高く飛ぶの。決して諦めないわ。どんなに世界が私に厳しくても、絶対に夢を諦めない。」

何メートルか後ろにナオミが立っていた。彼女はメグの言葉を盗み聞きしていたのだ。突然彼女は叫んだ。「ダメ。そんなの不公平よ。あなたはダメ。高く飛ぶのは私なのよ。私はスターになるために今までの人生をすべて費やして来たのよ。あなたじゃないわ。私よ。」

ナオミは泣き始めた。

メグは振り返って、ナオミが泣いているのを見た。

「え、あなた…どうして…？ 私が何をしたのか分からないけれど、もし嫌なことをしたんだったら、ごめんなさい。不公平と思うかもしれないけれど、これが私の人生でのたったひとつのチャンスなの。逃すことはできないのよ。」メグは言った。

「ダメよ。ダメ…私よ…私…」ナオミはグラグラとして倒れ込んだ。

メグは彼女の方へと走って行って彼女に話しかけた。「ねえ、大丈夫？ 聞こえる？」

しかし、返事はなかった。

【続く】

【第一巻終わり】

MEG the Miracle Idol

MEG
the Miracle Idol
Vol. 1
You can be a Star!

索引

Index

A

- [ ] a can of **green** tea 熟
  [gríːn] 47
- [ ] a **lot** 熟
  [lάt] 85
- [ ] a **lot** of ~ 熟
  [lάt] 25, 42, 85, 102
- [ ] a **lot** of times 熟
  [lάt] 73
- [ ] a piece of **bread** 熟
  [bréd] 33
- [ ] abandon 動
  [əbǽndən] 85
- [ ] accept 動
  [əksépt] 21, 95
- [ ] actor 名
  [ǽktər] 102
- [ ] add to ~ 熟
  [ǽd] 64
- [ ] admit 動
  [ədmít] 88
- [ ] adopt 動
  [ədάpt] 95
- [ ] advice 名
  [ədváis] 84
- [ ] after all 熟
  [ǽftər] 88
- [ ] after school 熟
  [ǽftər] 103
- [ ] album 名
  [ǽlbəm] 74
- [ ] all the **more** ~ 熟
  [mɔ́ːr] 113
- [ ] alley 名
  [ǽli] 38
- [ ] almost 副
  [ɔ́ːlmoust] 42
- [ ] alone 形
  [əlóun] 13, 85
- [ ] along 動
  [əlɔ́(ː)ŋ] 118
- [ ] already 副
  [ɔːlrédi] 59, 73, 84
- [ ] also 副
  [ɔ́ːlsou] 42, 58, 74, 90, 103
- [ ] although 接
  [ɔːlðóu] 9, 10, 13
- [ ] although ..... 接
  [ɔːlðóu] 11, 13, 102, 113
- [ ] and **stuff** 熟
  [stʌ́f] 78

- [ ] **anime** 名
  [ǽnəmei] 74
- [ ] **anime-related item** 熟
  [ǽnəmeirilétid áitəm] 74
- [ ] **announce** 動
  [ənáuns] 111
- [ ] **another** 形
  [ənʌ́ðər] 36, 42
- [ ] **anxious** 形
  [ǽŋkʃəs] 39
- [ ] **any more** 熟
  [èni mɔ́ːr] 25, 43
- [ ] **anymore** 副
  [ènimɔ́ːr] 65, 89
- [ ] **anyway** 副
  [éniwèi] 65, 84
- [ ] **anywhere** 副
  [éniwèər] 7
- [ ] **apartment** 名
  [əpάːrtmənt] 95
- [ ] **appearance** 名
  [əpíərəns] 83, 102
- [ ] **appreciate** 動
  [əpríːʃièit] 64, 104
- [ ] **area** 名
  [éəriə] 32
- [ ] **arm** 名
  [άːrm] 36
- [ ] **arrange** 動
  [əréindʒ] 12
- [ ] **as** ~ 前
  [əz, ǽz] 95
- [ ] **as** ··· **as** ~ 熟
  [əz, ǽz] 61
- [ ] **as** always 熟
  [əz, ǽz] 56
- [ ] **as much** as ..... 熟
  [mʌ́tʃ] 29
- [ ] **at all** 熟
  [ət ɔ́ːl] 98
- [ ] **at home** 熟
  [hóum] 7
- [ ] **at least** 熟
  [líːst] 33
- [ ] **at the same** time 熟
  [séim] 57
- [ ] **attack** 動
  [ətǽk] 87
- [ ] **attend** 動
  [əténd] 103, 110
- [ ] **attractive** 形
  [ətrǽktiv] 40

- ☐ **audience** 名
  [ɔ́ːdiəns] 82
- ☐ **aura** 名
  [ɔ́ːrə] 113
- ☐ **average** 形
  [ǽvərɪdʒ] 66
- ☐ **avoid** 動
  [əvɔ́ɪd] 26, 106
- ☐ **awkward** 形
  [ɔ́ːkwərd] 89

B

- ☐ **back alley** 熟
  [bǽk ǽli] 34, 87
- ☐ **backstage** 副
  [bǽksteɪdʒ] 91
- ☐ **ballet** 名
  [bæléɪ] 110
- ☐ **barely** 副
  [béərli] 6, 33
- ☐ **basement** 名
  [béɪsmənt] 48
- ☐ **bathhouse** 名
  [bǽθhàus] 26
- ☐ be **able** to V 熟
  [éɪbl] 29
- ☐ be at a **loss** for words 熟
  [lɔ́(ː)s] 88
- ☐ be **better** than ~ 熟
  [bétər] 47
- ☐ be **born** 熟
  [bɔ́ːrn] 6
- ☐ be **born** C 熟
  [bɔ́ːrn] 88
- ☐ be **born** into ~ 熟
  [bɔ́ːrn] 110
- ☐ be **full** of ~ 熟
  [fúl] 24
- ☐ be not **sure** if S V 熟
  [ʃúər] 9
- ☐ be **packed** with ~ 熟
  [pǽkt] 76
- ☐ be **stuffed** with ~ 熟
  [stʌ́ft] 22
- ☐ **beat** 動
  [bíːt] 7, 29, 52, 57, 84
- ☐ **beat** up ~ 熟
  [bíːt] 39
- ☐ **beauty parlor** 熟
  [bjúːti páːrlər] 58
- ☐ **because** ..... 接
  [bikɔ́ːz] 9, 42
- ☐ **behind** ~ 前
  [bɪhàɪnd] 50
- ☐ **believe** 動
  [bɪlíːv] 11, 17, 64
- ☐ **beside** ~ 前
  [bɪsàɪd] 46, 113
- ☐ **besides** 副
  [bɪsáɪdz] 40, 47, 65
- ☐ **beyond** ~ 前
  [biɑ̀ːnd] 9
- ☐ **bill** 名
  [bíl] 22, 25
- ☐ **blame** 動
  [bléɪm] 21
- ☐ **blanket** 名
  [blǽŋkət] 56
- ☐ **bleed** 動
  [blíːd] 83
- ☐ **blood** 名
  [blʌ́d] 39, 83
- ☐ **bluff** 動
  [blʌ́f] 46
- ☐ **blurry** 形
  [blə́ːri] 67
- ☐ **boot camp** 熟
  [búːt kǽmp] 102
- ☐ **bored** 形
  [bɔ́ːrd] 28
- ☐ **bow** 動
  [báu] 51
- ☐ **brace** oneself up 熟
  [bréɪs] 83
- ☐ **bright** 形
  [bráɪt] 82
- ☐ **bulldozer** 名
  [búldòuzər] 19
- ☐ **bully** 動
  [búli] 29
- ☐ **bury** 動
  [béri] 118
- ☐ **busily** 副
  [bízəli] 73
- ☐ **businesslike** 形
  [bíznəslàɪk] 78
- ☐ **button** 名
  [bʌ́tn] 40
- ☐ **buy** ~ at a sale 熟
  [báɪ] 28
- ☐ by **heart** 熟
  [háːrt] 11, 66
- ☐ by **oneself** 熟
  [wʌnsélf] 26

C

- [ ] **call** 動
  [kɔ́:l]   65, 94
- [ ] **calm** ~ down 熟
  [kɑ́:m]   43
- [ ] **camping gear** 熟
  [kǽmpiŋ gìər]   26
- [ ] can do **nothing** but V 熟
  [nʌ́θiŋ]   19
- [ ] cannot **help** oneself 熟
  [hélp]   115
- [ ] cannot **help** Ving 熟
  [hélp]   113
- [ ] **care** 動
  [kéər]   90
- [ ] **careful** 形
  [kéərfl]   28
- [ ] **catch** 動
  [kǽtʃ]   29
- [ ] **catch** up with ~ 熟
  [kǽtʃ]   48
- [ ] **cell phone** 熟
  [sél fòun]   39
- [ ] **CEO** 名
  [sí:ì:óu]   110
- [ ] **change** 名動
  [tʃéindʒ]   29, 107
- [ ] **change** into ~ 熟
  [tʃéindʒ]   58
- [ ] **chat** with ~ 熟
  [tʃǽt]   74
- [ ] **cheer** 名動
  [tʃíər]   77, 82
- [ ] **cheer** oneself up 熟
  [tʃíər]   13
- [ ] **choice** 名
  [tʃɔ́is]   29
- [ ] **city office** 熟
  [síti ɑ́:fəs]   18, 25, 52, 94
- [ ] **climb** up 熟
  [kláim]   79
- [ ] **closely** 副
  [klóusli]   53
- [ ] **clothes** 名
  [klóuz]   7, 58
- [ ] **coat** 名
  [kóut]   76
- [ ] **coin** 名
  [kɔ́in]   33, 87
- [ ] **cold** 形
  [kóuld]   106
- [ ] **collect** 動
  [kəlékt]   17, 28, 85
- [ ] **come back** 熟
  [kʌ́m bǽk]   12, 119
- [ ] **come** up 熟
  [kʌ́m]   32
- [ ] **come** up to ~ 熟
  [kʌ́m]   103
- [ ] **comic** book 熟
  [kɑ́:mik]   28, 85
- [ ] **common** 形
  [kɑ́:mən]   65
- [ ] **compared** to ~ 熟
  [kəmpéərd]   84
- [ ] **completely** 副
  [kəmplí:tli]   59
- [ ] **considering** ~ 前
  [kənsídəriŋ]   50
- [ ] **continue** 動
  [kəntínju:]   36
- [ ] **conversation** 名
  [kà:nvərséiʃən]   7, 73
- [ ] **convincing** 形
  [kənvínsiŋ]   40
- [ ] **cool** 形
  [kú:l]   84
- [ ] **cosmetics** 名
  [kɑ:zmétiks]   110
- [ ] **count** 動
  [káunt]   25
- [ ] **counter** 名
  [káuntər]   50
- [ ] **cover** 動
  [kʌ́vər]   67
- [ ] **cozy** 形
  [kóuzi]   26
- [ ] **crowd** 名
  [kráud]   79, 82
- [ ] **crowded** 形
  [kráudid]   76
- [ ] **cruel** 形
  [krú:əl]   17, 21, 24, 33
- [ ] **cry** 動
  [krái]   120
- [ ] **curious** 形
  [kjúəriəs]   115
- [ ] **curls** 名
  [kə́:rlz]   59
- [ ] **customer** 名
  [kʌ́stəmər]   74
- [ ] **cut** a class 熟
  [kʌ́t]   8

☐ cute 形	
[kjúːt]	97

D

☐ dangerous 形	
[déɪndʒərəs]	34, 47
☐ daughter 名	
[dɔ́ːtər]	95
☐ day off 熟	
[déɪ ɔ́(ː)f]	7
☐ dead 形	
[déd]	87, 107, 112
☐ deal 名	
[díːl]	39
☐ debt 名	
[dét]	17, 77
☐ debut 名	
[deɪbjúː]	68, 77, 102
☐ decide 動	
[dɪsáɪd]	97
☐ decide to V 熟	
[dɪsáɪd]	12, 26
☐ decoration 名	
[dèkəréɪʃən]	58
☐ delinquent 形	
[dɪlíŋkwənt]	87
☐ deny 動	
[dɪnáɪ]	106
☐ desperate 形	
[déspərət]	34
☐ detail 名	
[díːteɪl]	94
☐ devote 動	
[dɪvóut]	120
☐ diamond 名	
[dáɪmənd]	61, 64
☐ die 動	
[dáɪ]	87
☐ different from ~ 熟	
[dífərnt]	59
☐ dig 動	
[díg]	118
☐ district 名	
[dístrɪkt]	48
☐ doubt 動	
[dáut]	98
☐ downtown 名	
[dáuntáun]	24
☐ dream 動名	
[dríːm]	88, 110
☐ dream of ~ 熟	
[dríːm]	52, 74

☐ dreamy 形	
[dríːmi]	8
☐ drunk 形	
[dráŋk]	7
☐ drunken 形	
[dráŋkən]	34
☐ dye 動	
[dáɪ]	59
☐ dyed hair 熟	
[dáɪd hèər]	34

E

☐ elementary school 熟	
[èləméntəri skúːl]	6
☐ else 副	
[éls]	9
☐ emphasize 動	
[émfəsàɪz]	58
☐ empty 形	
[émpti]	13
☐ enough ~ to V 熟	
[ɪnʌ́f]	26
☐ (~) enough to V 熟	
[ɪnʌ́f]	33, 68
☐ envelope 名	
[énvəlòup]	21, 25
☐ escape 動	
[ɪskéɪp]	36
☐ escape from ~ 熟	
[ɪskéɪp]	8
☐ even 副	
[íːvn]	64
☐ even ~ 副	
[íːvn]	7, 88
☐ event 名	
[ɪvént]	57
☐ ever since ..... 熟	
[évər]	9
☐ every day 熟	
[évri]	103
☐ everything 代	
[évriθɪŋ]	43
☐ exceptional 形	
[ɪksépʃənl]	64
☐ excited 形	
[ɪksáɪtɪd]	52, 57
☐ existence 名	
[ɪgzístəns]	64
☐ experience 名	
[ɪkspíəriəns]	88
☐ explain 動	
[ɪkspléɪn]	94

□ eye contact 熟	
[áɪ kàːntækt]	106

F

□ fact 名	
[fækt]	21
□ factory 名	
[fǽktəri]	6
□ fair 形	
[féər]	120
□ fall 動	
[fɔ́ːl]	82, 120
□ fall flat on one's face 熟	
[fɔ́ːl flǽt]	82
□ falter 動	
[fɔ́ːltər]	120
□ fan 名	
[fæn]	90
□ fancy 形	
[fǽnsi]	8, 88
□ fashionable 形	
[fǽʃənəbl]	57
□ fashionably 動	
[fǽʃənəbli]	38
□ faster 動	
[fǽstər]	52, 57
□ fate 名	
[féɪt]	88
□ fault 名	
[fɔ́ːlt]	21
□ favor 名	
[féɪvər]	95
□ favorite 形	
[féɪvərət]	74
□ feel 動	
[fíːl]	95
□ feel C 熟	
[fíːl]	13, 17, 42, 57, 67
□ feel like ..... 熟	
[fíːl]	33
□ feel like Ving 熟	
[fíːl]	13, 53
□ feel O V 熟	
[fíːl]	48
□ feel O Ving 熟	
[fíːl]	52
□ fight 動	
[fáɪt]	39
□ figure 名	
[fígjər]	103
□ finally 動	
[fáɪnəli]	28, 52, 90

□ find 動	
[fáɪnd]	29, 107
□ find O C 熟	
[fáɪnd]	112
□ first 動	
[fə́ːrst]	40
□ fit 動	
[fít]	89
□ flood 動名	
[flʌ́d]	32, 87
□ flow 動	
[flóu]	22, 36
□ fly 動	
[fláɪ]	119
□ follow 動	
[fɑ́ːlou]	43, 57, 106, 118
□ for a long time 熟	
[lɔ́(ː)ŋ]	52
□ for a moment 熟	
[móumənt]	53, 82
□ for a while 熟	
[wáɪl]	85
□ for several seconds 熟	
[sévrəl]	89
□ for the first time 熟	
[fə́ːrst]	112
□ forever 動	
[fərévər]	30
□ forget 動	
[fərgét]	11, 84
□ foster parent 熟	
[fɔ́(ː)stər pèərənt]	94
□ free time 熟	
[fríː]	85
□ freedom 名	
[fríːdəm]	26
□ freeze 動	
[fríːz]	82
□ from behind 熟	
[bɪháɪnd]	21
□ front 名	
[frʌ́nt]	104
□ fun 名	
[fʌ́n]	53
□ funny 形	
[fʌ́ni]	72
□ furniture 名	
[fə́ːrnɪtʃər]	12

G

□ gambling place 熟	
[gǽmblɪŋ plèɪs]	7

- ☐ **gangster** 图
  [ɡǽŋstər]   13, 16
- ☐ **garbage** 图
  [ɡáːrbɪdʒ]   12, 28, 85
- ☐ **gaze** 動
  [ɡéɪz]   53
- ☐ **generous** 形
  [dʒénərəs]   95
- ☐ **get** C 動
  [ɡét]   39, 48
- ☐ **get** out of ~ 熟
  [ɡét]   76
- ☐ give a **sigh** of **relief** 熟
  [sáɪ] [rɪlíːf]   42
- ☐ **give** up 熟
  [ɡív]   119
- ☐ **glad** 形
  [ɡlǽd]   64
- ☐ **glasses** 图
  [ɡlǽsɪz]   32, 52, 57, 67, 76
- ☐ **go away** 熟
  [ɡòu əwéɪ]   39
- ☐ **go on** 熟
  [ɡòu áːn]   83
- ☐ go on the **stage** 熟
  [stéɪdʒ]   104
- ☐ **go out** 熟
  [ɡòu áut]   12
- ☐ go **through** ~ 熟
  [θrúː]   102
- ☐ **God** 图
  [ɡáːd]   88, 98
- ☐ **gone** 形
  [ɡɔ́(ː)n]   12, 16, 18, 21, 42
- ☐ **grab** 動
  [ɡrǽb]   36
- ☐ **grab** ~ 's heart 熟
  [ɡrǽb]   98
- ☐ **grave** 图
  [ɡréɪv]   119
- ☐ **gray** 形
  [ɡréɪ]   38, 76
- ☐ **ground** 图
  [ɡráund]   118
- ☐ **guilty** 形
  [ɡílti]   29

H

- ☐ **half** 图
  [hǽf]   26
- ☐ **half** an hour 熟
  [hǽf]   60, 73
- ☐ **hand** 動
  [hǽnd]   47
- ☐ **handkerchief** 图
  [hǽŋkərtʃɪf]   83, 112, 115
- ☐ **hate** oneself for ~ 熟
  [héɪt]   113
- ☐ have a **picture** taken 熟
  [píktʃər]   72
- ☐ **have** to V 熟
  [hǽf]   21, 32, 95, 102
- ☐ **help** 動
  [hélp]   6, 42
- ☐ **hero** 图
  [híːrou]   9
- ☐ **hide** 動
  [háɪd]   8
- ☐ **hit** 图動
  [hít]   11, 32
- ☐ **hold** 動
  [hóuld]   87
- ☐ **hold** up ~ 熟
  [hóuld]   39
- ☐ **hole** 图
  [hóul]   118
- ☐ **homeless** 形
  [hóumləs]   24, 59, 85
- ☐ **horse race** 熟
  [hɔ́ːrs rèɪs]   7
- ☐ **how** to V 熟
  [háu]   25, 72, 104
- ☐ **however** 副
  [hauévər]   87
- ☐ **however** ..... 副
  [hauévər]   119
- ☐ **huge** 形
  [hjúːdʒ]   50, 79
- ☐ **hurt** 動
  [hə́ːrt]   38, 84

I

- ☐ **if** ..... 接
  [íf]   25, 39, 47, 77, 98, 120
- ☐ **ignore** 動
  [ɪɡnɔ́ːr]   106
- ☐ **imitate** 動
  [ímətèɪt]   9
- ☐ **important** 形
  [ɪmpɔ́ːrtnt]   40
- ☐ **impossible** 形
  [ɪmpáːsəbl]   11
- ☐ **impress** 動
  [ɪmprés]   68

- ☐ in a **daze**
  [déɪz]   21
- ☐ **in** fact
  [ín]   111
- ☐ **in front** of ~
  [fɾʌ́nt]   48
- ☐ in one's **thirties**
  [θə́ːrtiːz]   38
- ☐ in **public**
  [pʌ́blɪk]   66
- ☐ in **tears**
  [tíərz]   89
- ☐ in the **future**
  [fjúːtʃər]   74, 102
- ☐ **including** ~
  [ɪnklúːdɪŋ]   50, 67
- ☐ **instructor**
  [ɪnstrʌ́ktər]   103
- ☐ **intently**
  [ɪnténtli]   52
- ☐ **interfere**
  [ìntərfíər]   39
- ☐ **introduce**
  [ìntrəd(j)úːs]   104
- ☐ **introduce** to A B
  [ìntrəd(j)úːs]   79
- ☐ it can't be **helped**
  [hélpt]   88

J

- ☐ **jealous**
  [dʒéləs]   106, 113
- ☐ **jersey**
  [dʒə́ːrzi]   19, 32, 56
- ☐ **join**
  [dʒɔ́ɪn]   7
- ☐ **junior high school**
  [dʒúːnjər háɪ skùːl]   8

K

- ☐ **keep** A out of B
  [kíːp]   94
- ☐ **keep** O C
  [kíːp]   95
- ☐ **keep** Ving
  [kíːp]   22, 38, 84, 95
- ☐ **kid**
  [kíd]   84
- ☐ **kill**
  [kíl]   36
- ☐ **kind**
  [káɪnd]   95
- ☐ **kind** of
  [káɪnd]   47, 85
- ☐ **kneel** down
  [níːl]   119
- ☐ **knife**
  [náɪf]   38, 87
- ☐ **knock**
  [nάːk]   13

L

- ☐ **lace** one's **fingers**
  [léɪs wʌ́nz fíŋgərz]   119
- ☐ **land**
  [lǽnd]   17
- ☐ **lap**
  [lǽp]   73
- ☐ **last**
  [lǽst]   89
- ☐ **Laundromat**
  [lɔ́ːndrəmæt]   28
- ☐ **lawyer**
  [lɔ́ɪər]   94
- ☐ **leave**
  [líːv]   32
- ☐ **leave** ~ **alone**
  [líːv əlóun]   36
- ☐ **legal**
  [líːgl]   18
- ☐ **legal office**
  [líːgl άːfəs]   94
- ☐ **lend**
  [lénd]   17
- ☐ **lens**
  [lénz]   8
- ☐ **let** ~ V
  [lét]   43
- ☐ **lie**
  [láɪ]   112
- ☐ **life**
  [láɪf]   9, 11, 21, 24, 33, 87
- ☐ **lifestyle**
  [láɪfstàɪl]   29
- ☐ **light**
  [láɪt]   82
- ☐ **like** ~
  [láɪk]   11, 16, 28, 30, 34, 60, 66, 72, 84, 104, 110, 113
- ☐ **listen** to ~
  [lísn]   40
- ☐ **live**
  [lív]   17, 25
- ☐ **local store**
  [lóukl stɔ́ːr]   29

☐ **lonely** 形	
[lóunli]	13

☐ **look** at ~ 熟	
[lúk]	24, 59, 118

☐ **look** away 熟	
[lúk]	106

☐ **look** C 熟	
[lúk]	38, 58, 110

☐ **look like** ~ 熟	
[lúk láik]	8, 13, 47, 58, 72

☐ **look** up 熟	
[lúk]	24

☐ **lose** 動	
[lú:z]	26, 34, 43, 65, 85, 120

☐ **loud** 形	
[láud]	19, 77

☐ **luxurious** 形	
[lʌgʒúəriəs]	48

☐ **lyrics** 名	
[líriks]	66

M

☐ **magazine** 名	
[mǽgəzìːn]	85

☐ **maid cafe** 熟	
[méid kæféi]	74

☐ **main street** 熟	
[méin strìːt]	40, 44

☐ **make** a call 熟	
[méik]	73

☐ make a **debut** 熟	
[deibjúː]	103, 111

☐ make a **mistake** 熟	
[məstéik]	106

☐ **make** O C 熟	
[méik]	43

☐ **make** O V 熟	
[méik]	19, 64

☐ **make** up for ~ 熟	
[méik]	53

☐ **manage** to V 熟	
[mǽnidʒ]	32, 88

☐ many pieces of **furniture** 熟	
[fə́ːrnitʃər]	12

☐ **material** 名	
[mətíəriəl]	68

☐ **maybe** 副	
[méibi]	88

☐ **MC** 名	
[èmsíː]	78

☐ **mean** 動	
[míːn]	16, 51

☐ **mecca** 名	
[mékə]	74

☐ **messy** 形	
[mési]	8, 56

☐ **metal** 名	
[métl]	58

☐ **middle-aged** 形	
[mídléidʒd]	13, 72

☐ **might** have to V 熟	
[máit]	66

☐ **miracle** 名	
[mírəkl]	88

☐ **mirror** 名	
[mírər]	59

☐ **miserable** 形	
[mízərəbl]	9, 11

☐ **misery** 名	
[mízəri]	89

☐ **missing** 形	
[mísiŋ]	94

☐ **more than** ~ 熟	
[mɔ́ːr ðn]	42

☐ **most of** ~ 熟	
[móust]	11

☐ **move** 動	
[múːv]	97

☐ **must** have Vpp 熟	
[mʌ́st]	119

N

☐ **nap** 名	
[nǽp]	48

☐ **navy suit** 熟	
[néivi sùːt]	73

☐ **nearby** 副	
[níərbái]	28, 118

☐ **need** to V 熟	
[níːd]	17, 88, 102, 112

☐ **nervous** 形	
[nə́ːrvəs]	57, 67, 78, 89, 104

☐ **nervousness** 名	
[nə́ːrvəsnəs]	83

☐ **next** to ~ 熟	
[nékst]	111

☐ **nicely** 副	
[náisli]	38, 60

☐ **noise** 名	
[nɔ́iz]	19

☐ **noisy** 形	
[nɔ́izi]	12

☐ **normal** 形	
[nɔ́ːrml]	72

157

- ☐ **nose** 图
  [nóuz]   83
- ☐ not have **anything** to do with ~ 熟
  [éniθìŋ]   52
- ☐ not **only** A but **also** B 熟
  [óunli] [ɔ́:lsou]   113
- ☐ **nowhere** 副
  [nóuwèər]   18, 43, 87
- ☐ **number** 图
  [nʌ́mbər]   11

O

- ☐ **occasion** 图
  [əkéiʒən]   89
- ☐ of **course** 熟
  [kɔ́:rs]   46
- ☐ off **key** 熟
  [kí:]   90
- ☐ **offend** 動
  [əfénd]   120
- ☐ **offer** 图
  [ɔ́(:)fər]   95, 99
- ☐ **official** 形
  [əfíʃəl]   102
- ☐ **officially** 副
  [əfíʃəli]   94
- ☐ on **weekdays** 熟
  [wí:kdèiz]   103
- ☐ on **weekends** 熟
  [wí:kèndz]   103
- ☐ **once** ..... 接
  [wʌ́ns]   26
- ☐ one **after** another 熟
  [ǽftər]   89
- ☐ one's **way** of talking 熟
  [wéi]   16
- ☐ **oneself** 代
  [wʌnsélf]   9, 21
- ☐ or **whatever** 熟
  [wʌtévər]   18
- ☐ **other** than ~ 熟
  [ʌ́ðər ðn]   25
- ☐ **outside** 副
  [àutsáid]   19
- ☐ **outside** ~ 前
  [àutsáid]   50
- ☐ **over** 副
  [óuvər]   78
- ☐ **overhear** 動
  [òuvərhíər]   119
- ☐ **owe** 動
  [óu]   85
- ☐ **own** 動
  [óun]   6, 47, 77, 102

P

- ☐ pachinko **parlor** 熟
  [pá:rlər]   7
- ☐ **pale** 形
  [péil]   21
- ☐ **park** 動
  [pá:rk]   40, 44, 50
- ☐ **parking lot** 熟
  [pá:rkiŋ là:t]   73
- ☐ **pass** 動
  [pǽs | pá:s]   32
- ☐ **passenger seat** 熟
  [pǽsəndʒər sì:t]   46
- ☐ **pat** 動
  [pǽt]   21
- ☐ **pay** 動
  [péi]   6, 17
- ☐ **perfect** 形
  [pə́:rfikt]   68
- ☐ **perfectly** 副
  [pə́:rfiktli]   18
- ☐ **perspire** 動
  [pərspáiər]   104
- ☐ **photographer** 图
  [fətá:grəfər]   72
- ☐ **pick** 動
  [pík]   84
- ☐ **pick** on ~ 熟
  [pík]   8
- ☐ **pick** up ~ 熟
  [pík]   29, 42
- ☐ **pigeon** 图
  [pídʒən]   112
- ☐ **pile** 图
  [páil]   12, 28, 85
- ☐ **pinstripe** 图
  [pínstràip]   58
- ☐ **place** 图
  [pléis]   25
- ☐ **pop star** 熟
  [pá:p stá:r]   9, 61, 95, 102
- ☐ **popular idol** 熟
  [pá:pjələr áidl]   9
- ☐ **portable** 形
  [pɔ́:rtəbl]   28
- ☐ **pose** 動
  [póuz]   72
- ☐ **potential** 图
  [pəténʃəl]   97

☐ **practice** Ving 🏷 [præktɪs]	11
☐ **praise** 🏷 [préɪz]	64
☐ **prepare** 🏷 [prɪpéər]	57
☐ **prepare** for ~ 🏷 [prɪpéər]	111
☐ **prestigious** 🏷 [prestíːdʒəs]	103
☐ **pretty well** 🏷 [príti wél]	9
☐ **probably** 🏷 [prάːbəbli]	26
☐ **problem** 🏷 [prάːbləm]	17
☐ **produce** 🏷 [prəd(j)úːs]	6
☐ **professional** 🏷🏷 [prəféʃənl]	72, 84
☐ **propose** 🏷 [prəpóuz]	39
☐ **public** 🏷 [pʌ́blɪk]	102
☐ **pure** 🏷 [pjúər]	97
☐ **push** 🏷 [púʃ]	40
☐ **put** 🏷 [pút]	119
☐ **put** on ~ 🏷 [pút]	57

Q

☐ **quiet** 🏷 [kwάɪət]	38
☐ **quite** 🏷 [kwάɪt]	33, 78

R

☐ **rage** 🏷 [réɪdʒ]	112
☐ **rarely** ..... 🏷 [réərli]	6
☐ **react** 🏷 [riǽkt]	115
☐ **reaction** 🏷 [riǽkʃən]	97
☐ **real** 🏷 [ríːjəl]	53, 61
☐ **really** 🏷 [ríːli]	50

☐ **reception desk** 🏷 [rɪsépʃən dèsk]	50
☐ **receptionist** 🏷 [rɪsépʃənist]	50
☐ **refine** 🏷 [rɪfάɪn]	97, 102
☐ **reflect** 🏷 [rɪflékt]	118
☐ **refrigerator** 🏷 [rɪfrídʒərèɪtər]	13
☐ **regret** 🏷 [rɪgrét]	89
☐ **regular** 🏷 [régjələr]	102
☐ **relax** 🏷 [rɪlǽks]	72
☐ **reliable** 🏷 [rɪlάɪəbl]	78
☐ **relieve** 🏷 [rɪlíːv]	38
☐ **remember** 🏷 [rɪmémbər]	25, 33, 56
☐ **reply** 🏷 [rɪplάɪ]	16
☐ **represent** 🏷 [rèprɪzént]	51
☐ **respond** 🏷 [rɪspάːnd]	87
☐ **response** 🏷 [rɪspάːns]	122
☐ **right** 🏷🏷 [rάɪt]	18, 61
☐ **right** away 🏷 [rάɪt]	40
☐ **right now** 🏷 [rάɪt náu]	97
☐ **rise** to one's feet 🏷 [rάɪz]	82
☐ **riverbank** 🏷 [rívərbæ̀ŋk]	26, 118
☐ **riverside** 🏷 [rívərsàɪd]	28
☐ **roll** up 🏷 [róul]	19
☐ **rough** 🏷 [rʌ́f]	97
☐ **round** 🏷 [rάund]	119
☐ **rubble** 🏷 [rʌ́bl]	19
☐ **rule** 🏷 [rúːl]	26

- ☐ **run away** 熟
  [rʌ́n əwéɪ] 16
- ☐ **run** into ~ 熟
  [rʌ́n] 38
- ☐ **run short of money** 熟
  [rʌ́n ʃɔ́ːrt əv mʌ́ni] 28

S

- ☐ **sad** 形
  [sǽd] 17, 34
- ☐ **sadly** 副
  [sǽdli] 33
- ☐ **Saturday** 名
  [sǽtərdeɪ] 74
- ☐ **save** 動
  [séɪv] 88
- ☐ **say** hi to ~ 熟
  [séɪ] 104
- ☐ **say** to oneself 熟
  [séɪ] 24
- ☐ **scared** 形
  [skéərd] 16
- ☐ **scream** 動
  [skríːm] 36, 38
- ☐ **second** 形
  [sékənd] 33
- ☐ **secret** 名
  [síːkrət] 95
- ☐ **secretly** 副
  [síːkrətli] 112, 118
- ☐ **seem** C 熟
  [síːm] 106
- ☐ **seem** to be C 熟
  [síːm] 38
- ☐ **seldom** ..... 副
  [séldəm] 7
- ☐ **self-confidence** 名
  [sèlfkάːnfədəns] 64
- ☐ **September** 名
  [septémbər] 32
- ☐ **serious** 形
  [síəriəs] 52, 98
- ☐ **serve** 動
  [sə́ːrv] 74
- ☐ **set** up ~ 熟
  [sét] 26
- ☐ **shine** 動
  [ʃáɪn] 64
- ☐ **shoplift** 動
  [ʃάːplìft] 29
- ☐ **should** have Vpp 熟
  [ʃúd] 98
- ☐ **sign** 名
  [sáɪn] 50
- ☐ **silence** 名
  [sáɪləns] 89
- ☐ **silent** 形
  [sáɪlənt] 89
- ☐ **silly** 形
  [síli] 83
- ☐ **silver-framed glasses** 熟
  [sílvərfrèɪmd glǽsɪz] 8
- ☐ **since** ..... 接
  [síns] 85, 104, 110
- ☐ **sit** down 熟
  [sít] 118
- ☐ **situation** 名
  [sìtʃuéɪʃən] 39
- ☐ **skill** 名
  [skíl] 102
- ☐ **skyscraper** 名
  [skάɪskrèɪpər] 48
- ☐ **sleepy** 形
  [slíːpi] 48
- ☐ **slim** 形
  [slím] 111
- ☐ **smart** 形
  [smάːrt] 110
- ☐ **smash** 動
  [smǽʃ] 19
- ☐ **smile** 動
  [smάɪl] 78, 91, 106
- ☐ **so** 副接
  [sóu] 52, 65
- ☐ **somehow** 副
  [sʌ́mhàu] 95
- ☐ **something** to drink 熟
  [sʌ́mθìŋ] 43
- ☐ **sorry** 形
  [sάːri] 42, 60
- ☐ **sound** C 熟
  [sáund] 40, 78
- ☐ **soy sauce** 名
  [sɔ́ɪ sɔ̀ːs] 13
- ☐ **spend** 動
  [spénd] 12, 26, 72, 111
- ☐ **spend** 時間 Ving 熟
  [spénd] 13
- ☐ **stage** 名
  [stéɪdʒ] 79
- ☐ **stage name** 熟
  [stéɪdʒ nèɪm] 65
- ☐ **stand** up 熟
  [stǽnd] 53, 89, 119

- ☐ **stick** 名
  [stík] 118
- ☐ **still** 副
  [stíl] 56
- ☐ **stone** 名
  [stóun] 119
- ☐ **story** 名
  [stɔ́:ri] 77
- ☐ **straight** 形
  [stréɪt] 110
- ☐ **strange** 形
  [stréɪndʒ] 25, 33, 60
- ☐ **stranger** 名
  [stréɪndʒər] 16
- ☐ **strict** 形
  [stríkt] 26
- ☐ **stunned** 形
  [stʌ́nd] 61, 66
- ☐ **style** 動
  [stáɪl] 59
- ☐ **stylist** 名
  [stáɪlɪst] 57
- ☐ **suburb** 名
  [sʌ́bə:rb] 6
- ☐ **such** 形
  [sʌ́tʃ] 17
- ☐ **suddenly** 副
  [sʌ́dnli] 34, 89, 111
- ☐ **sunset** 名
  [sʌ́nsèt] 118
- ☐ **support** 動
  [səpɔ́:rt] 90
- ☐ **sure** 形
  [ʃúər] 83
- ☐ **surface** 名
  [sɔ́:rfəs] 118
- ☐ **surprised** 形
  [sərpráɪzd] 59
- ☐ **surprisingly** 副
  [sərpráɪzɪŋli] 29
- ☐ **surround** 動
  [səráund] 34
- ☐ **swallow** 動
  [swɑ́:lou] 32

T

- ☐ take a **shower** 熟
  [ʃáuər] 58
- ☐ **take** ~ off 熟
  [téɪk] 52, 67, 76
- ☐ **take** on ~ 熟
  [téɪk] 38
- ☐ **take out** ~ 熟
  [tèɪk áut] 12, 25, 32, 40, 83, 118
- ☐ take the **elevator** 熟
  [éləvèɪtər] 50
- ☐ **take** the pictures 熟
  [téɪk] 72
- ☐ **talent agency** 熟
  [tǽlənt éɪdʒənsi] 50
- ☐ **talk** about ~ 熟
  [tɔ́:k] 7, 65, 85
- ☐ **talk** to ~ 熟
  [tɔ́:k] 72, 122
- ☐ **talk** with ~ 熟
  [tɔ́:k] 6
- ☐ **taste** 名
  [téɪst] 53
- ☐ **tattered jeans** 熟
  [tǽtərd dʒí:nz] 8
- ☐ **tattoo** 名
  [tætú:] 34
- ☐ **tear** 名
  [tíər] 21, 24, 33
- ☐ **tear** down ~ 熟
  [téər] 18
- ☐ **terrible** 形
  [térəbl] 113
- ☐ **thank** you for ~ 熟
  [θǽŋk] 43, 83
- ☐ **thankful** to ~ 熟
  [θǽŋkfl] 42
- ☐ the **kind** of ~ 熟
  [káɪnd] 59
- ☐ the **police** 熟
  [pəlí:s] 94
- ☐ the **very** + 最上級 熟
  [véri] 111
- ☐ the **world** 熟
  [wɔ́:rld] 8
- ☐ **theme park** 熟
  [θí:m pà:rk] 7
- ☐ **then** 副
  [ðén] 19, 43, 58, 65, 73
- ☐ there's no **way** (that) ..... 熟
  [wéɪ] 95
- ☐ **thick** 形
  [θík] 8
- ☐ **think** about ~ 熟
  [θíŋk] 25, 43
- ☐ **think** to oneself 熟
  [θíŋk] 99, 112
- ☐ **third** 形
  [θɔ́:rd] 38

161

- ☐ **thousands** of times 熟
  [θáuzn*dz*] — 11
- ☐ **through** ~ 前
  [θrúː] — 8, 74
- ☐ **throw** 動
  [θróu] — 40
- ☐ **tight** 形
  [táɪt] — 58
- ☐ **tired** 形
  [táɪərd] — 48
- ☐ **together** 副
  [təɡéðər] — 6
- ☐ **too** ~ 副
  [túː] — 18, 65, 82
- ☐ **totally** 副
  [tóutəli] — 66
- ☐ **tough** 形
  [tʌ́f] — 119
- ☐ **toward** ~ 前
  [tɔ́ːrd] — 82
- ☐ **toy** 名
  [tɔ́ɪ] — 8
- ☐ **trail** 名
  [tréɪl] — 118
- ☐ **train** 動
  [tréɪn] — 111
- ☐ **treat** 動
  [tríːt] — 60
- ☐ **tremble** 動
  [trémbl] — 19, 112
- ☐ **trip** on ~ 熟
  [trɪ́p] — 82
- ☐ **true** 形
  [trúː] — 33, 47
- ☐ **trust** 動
  [trʌ́st] — 47
- ☐ **try** to V 熟
  [tráɪ] — 36, 78, 106
- ☐ **turn** 名
  [tə́ːrn] — 78
- ☐ **turn around** 熟
  [tə́ːrn əráund] — 21, 120
- ☐ **TV personality** 名
  [pə̀ːrsənǽləti] — 50
- ☐ **typhoon season** 熟
  [taɪfúːn sìːzn] — 32
- ☐ **typical** 形
  [típɪkl] — 61, 67

U

- ☐ **uncomfortable** 形
  [ʌnkʌ́mftəbl] — 58
- ☐ **unfair** 形
  [ʌnféər] — 112, 120
- ☐ **uniform** 名
  [júːnəfɔ̀ːrm] — 58, 74
- ☐ **unlike** ~ 前
  [ʌnláɪk] — 7
- ☐ **unlocked** 形
  [ʌnlɑ́ːkt] — 12
- ☐ **unlucky** 形
  [ʌnlʌ́ki] — 88
- ☐ **upset** 形
  [ʌpsét] — 17, 83
- ☐ **utter** 動
  [ʌ́tər] — 19

V

- ☐ **variety show** 名
  [vəráɪəti ʃóu] — 61
- ☐ **vending machine** 名
  [véndɪŋ məʃìːn] — 29
- ☐ **veranda** 名
  [vərǽndə] — 112
- ☐ **video arcade** 名
  [vídiòu ɑːrkèɪd] — 29, 87

W

- ☐ **wage** 名
  [wéɪdʒ] — 6
- ☐ **waist** 名
  [wéɪst] — 58
- ☐ **wait a moment** 熟
  [móumənt] — 56
- ☐ **wait** for ~ 熟
  [wéɪt] — 12
- ☐ **wake** up 熟
  [wéɪk] — 18, 56
- ☐ **walk around** 熟
  [wɔ́ːk əráund] — 24
- ☐ **wallet** 名
  [wɑ́ːlət] — 40
- ☐ **want** to be ~ 熟
  [wɑ́nt] — 11
- ☐ **want** to V 熟
  [wɑ́nt] — 25, 53, 65, 85, 102, 119
- ☐ **wash** away 熟
  [wɑ́ːʃ] — 87
- ☐ **way** 副
  [wéɪ] — 61
- ☐ **wear** 動
  [wéər] — 8, 56, 76, 82
- ☐ **weekly** 形
  [wíːkli] — 6

- ☐ **well** up 熟
  [wél] 21
- ☐ **when** ..... 接
  [wén] 6, 11, 16, 18, 24, 57, 84, 104, 111, 118
- ☐ **whisper** to ~ 熟
  [wíspər] 106, 113
- ☐ **white flu mask** 熟
  [wáɪt flúː mæ̀sk] 76
- ☐ **whole** 形
  [hóul] 33
- ☐ **whole day** 熟
  [hóul dèɪ] 12
- ☐ **wipe away** ~ 熟
  [wáɪp əwéɪ] 25
- ☐ **wipe** ~ off 熟
  [wáɪp] 83
- ☐ **wish** ..... 動
  [wíʃ] 72, 87, 113
- ☐ **wish** to V 熟
  [wíʃ] 9, 30
- ☐ **wonder** 動
  [wʌ́ndər] 56
- ☐ **wooden** 形
  [wúdn] 118
- ☐ **worried** 形
  [wɔ́ːrid] 39
- ☐ **worse** 形
  [wɔ́ːrs] 39
- ☐ **worthy** 形
  [wɔ́ːrði] 60
- ☐ would **like** to V 熟
  [láɪk] 79, 104
- ☐ **wrap** 動
  [ræp] 112, 115

Y

- ☐ **yell** 動
  [jél] 89, 115
- ☐ **yell** at ~ 熟
  [jél] 7

MEG the Miracle Idol

●大学受験 英文多読シリーズ

ミラクルアイドルメグ Vol.1

発行日:2013年3月4日　初版発行
　　　 2014年12月22日　第3版発行

著　者:安河内哲也
発行者:永瀬昭幸

編集担当:村本悠
発行所:株式会社ナガセ
　　　〒180-0003　東京都武蔵野市吉祥寺南1-29-2
　　　出版事業部(東進ブックス)
　　　TEL:0422-70-7456 ／ FAX:0422-70-7457
　　　URL:http://www.toshin.com/books/
　　　(本書を含む東進ブックスの最新情報は上記「WEB書店」をご覧ください)

カバー・本文デザイン:LIGHTNING
イラスト:碧風羽
執筆協力・校閲:Matthew Radich／Mickey Acorn／Nadia McKechnie
翻訳・編集協力:山越友子／向山美紗子

DTP:株式会社秀文社
印刷・製本:日経印刷株式会社
音声収録・編集:財団法人 英語教育協議会(ELEC)／株式会社エスプリズム
音声出演:日髙のり子／Rachel Walzer

※落丁・乱丁本は着払いにて小社出版事業部宛にお送りください。新本にお取り替えいたします。
※本書を無断で複写・複製・転載することを禁じます。

Tetsuya Yasukochi 2013 Printed in Japan
ISBN9784-89085-560-5　C7382

── 音声ダウンロードサイト ──

http://www.toshin.com/books/

※音声ダウンロードの際は、下記のパスワードが必要です。詳細は上記のサイトをご参照ください。

Password : BHs5QfRW
（エフ）

東進ブックス

編集部より

この本を読み終えた君に オススメの3冊！

ALLマンガ！ 安河内哲也のリアル授業を完全漫画化。英語の勉強法の悩みはこの1冊で全て解決できる!

「ゼロ」からわかる超定番の英文法講義。英文法を中学レベルから一気にマスターしたい人にオススメ。

ミラクルアイドルメグ2巻！いよいよ後編クライマックスへ突入。楽しみながら、すらすら英語を読んじゃおう!

体験授業

この本を書いた講師の授業を受けてみませんか？

東進では有名実力講師陣の授業を無料で体験できる『体験授業』を行っています。「わかる」授業、「完璧に」理解できるシステム、そして最後まで「頑張れる」雰囲気を実際に体験してください。

※1講座(90分×1回)を受講できます。
※お電話でご予約ください。
　連絡先は付録9ページをご覧ください。
※お友達同士でも受講できます。

安河内先生の主な担当講座　※2014年度
「有名大突破！戦略英語解法」 など

東進の合格の秘訣が次ページに

合格の秘訣1 全国屈指の実力講師陣

ベストセラー著者のなんと7割が東進の講師陣!!

東進ハイスクール・東進衛星予備校では、そうそうたる講師陣が君を熱く指導する!

本気で実力をつけたいと思うなら、やはり根本から理解させてくれる一流講師の授業を受けることが大切です。東進の講師は、日本全国から選りすぐられた大学受験のプロフェッショナル。何万人もの受験生を志望校合格へ導いてきたエキスパート達です。

全国の受験生から絶大な支持を得る「東進ブックス」

英語

安河内 哲也 先生 [英語]
数えきれないほどの受験生の偏差値を改造、難関大へ送り込む!

今井 宏 先生 [英語]
予備校界のカリスマ講師。君に驚きと満足、そして合格を与えてくれる

福崎 伍郎 先生 [英語]
その鮮やかすぎる解法で受験生の圧倒的な支持を集める超実力講師!

渡辺 勝彦 先生 [英語]
「スーパー速読法」で、難解な英文も一発で理解させる超実力講師!

大岩 秀樹 先生 [英語]
情熱と若さあふれる授業で、知らず知らずのうちに英語が得意教科に!

宮崎 尊 先生 [英語]
雑誌「TIME」の翻訳など、英語界でその名を馳せる有名実力講師!

数学

志田 晶 先生 [数学]
数学科実力講師は、わかりやすさを徹底的に追求する

長岡 恭史 先生 [数学]
受講者からは理Ⅲを含む東大や国立医学部など超難関大合格者が続出

沖田 一希 先生 [数学]
短期間で数学力を徹底的に養成。知識を統一・体系化する!

付録 1

WEBで体験

東進ドットコムで授業を体験できます！
実力講師陣の詳しい紹介や、各教科の学習アドバイスも読めます。
www.toshin.com/teacher/

国語

板野 博行 先生 [現代文・古文]
「わかる」国語は君のやる気を生み出す特効薬

出口 汪 先生 [現代文] 
ミスター驚異の現代文。数々のベストセラー著者としても超有名！

吉野 敬介 先生 [古文] ＜客員講師＞
予備校界の超大物が東進に登場。ドラマチックで熱い講義を体験せよ

富井 健二 先生 [古文]
ビジュアル解説で古文を簡単明快に解き明かす実力講師

三羽 邦美 先生 [古文・漢文] 
縦横無尽な知識に裏打ちされた立体的な授業に、グングン引き込まれる！

樋口 裕一 先生 [小論文] ＜客員講師＞
小論文指導の第一人者。著書「頭がいい人、悪い人の話し方」は250万部突破！

理科

橋元 淳一郎 先生 [物理]
橋元流の解法は君の脳に衝撃を与える！

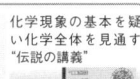

鎌田 真彰 先生 [化学]
化学現象の基本を疑い化学全体を見通す"伝説の講義"

田部 眞哉 先生 [生物]
全国の受験生が絶賛するその授業は、わかりやすさそのもの！

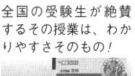

地歴公民

荒巻 豊志 先生 [世界史]
"受験世界史に荒巻あり"と言われる超実力人気講師

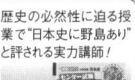

金谷 俊一郎 先生 [日本史] 
入試頻出事項に的を絞った「表解板書」は圧倒的な信頼を得る！

野島 博之 先生 [日本史] 
歴史の必然性に迫る授業で"日本史に野島あり"と評される実力講師！

村瀬 哲史 先生 [地理]
「そうだったのか！」と気づき理解できる。考えることがおもしろくなってくる授業

清水 雅博 先生 [公民]
全国の政経受験者が絶賛のベストセラー講師！

付録 2

合格の秘訣2 革新的な学習システム

東進には、第一志望合格に必要なすべての要素を満たし、抜群の合格実績を生み出す学習システムがあります。

ITを駆使した最先端の勉強法
高速学習

一人ひとりのレベル・目標にぴったりの授業

東進はすべての授業を映像化しています。その数およそ1万種類。これらの授業を個別に受講できるので、一人ひとりのレベル・目標に合った学習が可能です。1.4倍速受講ができるほか自宅のパソコンからも受講できるので、今までにない効率的な学習が実現します。

1年分の授業を最短2週間から3カ月で受講

従来の予備校は、毎週1回の授業。しかし、高速学習ならこれを毎日受講することができます。1年分の授業が最短2週間から3カ月程度で終了。先取り学習や苦手科目の克服、勉強と部活との両立が可能になります。

現役合格者の声

早稲田大学 政治経済学部
大坪 元くん

中学生のころから苦手だった英語を克服するため、高2の3月に東進に入学。自分のペースでどんどん高速学習できるので、限られた時間の中でも英語を基礎からやり直すことができました。

先取りカリキュラム

	高1	高2	高3
東進の学習方法	高1生の学習	高2生の学習	高3生の学習 → 受験勉強
	数学I・A	数学II・B	数学III
	高2のうちに受験全範囲を修了する		
従来の学習方法（公立高校の場合）	高1生の学習	高2生の学習	高3生の学習
	数学I・A	数学II・B	数学III

目標まで一歩ずつ確実に
スモールステップ・パーフェクトマスター

基礎から着実に難関レベルに到達できる

自分に合ったレベルから始め、確実に力を伸ばすことが可能です。「簡単すぎる」「難しすぎる」といった無駄がなく、志望校へ最短距離で進みます。また、授業後には「確認テスト」や「講座修了判定テスト」で理解してから先に進むので、わからない部分を残すことはありません。自分の学習成果を細かく確認しながら、着実に力をつけることができます。

現役合格者の声

東京大学 文科I類
永沢 はなさん

東進では授業の後に確認テストがあります。毎回、満点をとることを目指して授業で学習した範囲をくまなく復習することで、知識を漏れなく身につけることができました。

パーフェクトマスターのしくみ

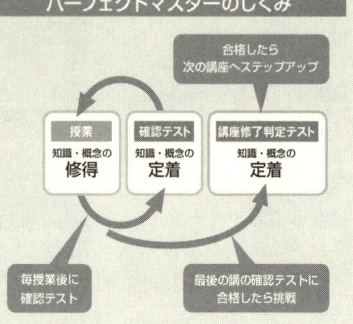

合格したら次の講座へステップアップ

授業（知識・概念の修得）→ 確認テスト（知識・概念の定着）→ 講座修了判定テスト（知識・概念の定着）

- 毎授業後に確認テスト
- 最後の講の確認テストに合格したら挑戦

付録 3

個別説明会

全国の東進ハイスクール・東進衛星予備校の各校舎にて実施しています。
※お問い合わせ先は、付録9ページをご覧ください。

徹底的に学力の土台を固める

高速基礎マスター講座

　高速基礎マスター講座は「知識」と「トレーニング」の両面から、科学的かつ効率的に短期間で基礎学力を徹底的に身につけるための講座です。文法事項や重要事項を単元別・分野別にひとつずつ完成させていくことができます。インターネットを介してオンラインで利用できるため、校舎だけでなく、自宅のパソコンやスマートフォンアプリで学習することも可能です。

現役合格者の声

大阪大学 工学部
原田 樹くん

　東進で部活と勉強を両立していた野球部の先輩の紹介で入学。「高速基礎マスター講座」の活用により、センター試験に必須の英単語など、基礎知識を素早く、手軽に覚えられました。

東進公式スマートフォンアプリ
■東進式マスター登場!
（英単語／英熟語／英文法／基本例文）

スマートフォンアプリですき間時間も徹底活用!

1）スモールステップ・パーフェクトマスター!
頻出度（重要度）の高い英単語から始め、1つのSTEP(計100語)を完全修得すると次のSTEPに進めるようになります。

2）自分の英単語力が一目でわかる!
トップ画面に「修得語数・修得率」をメーター表示。
自分が今何語修得しているのか、どこを優先的に学習すべきなのか一目でわかります。

3）「覚えていない単語」だけを集中攻略できる!
未修得の単語、または「My単語（自分でチェック登録した単語）」だけをテストする出題設定が可能です。
すでに覚えている単語を何度も学習するような無駄を省き、効率良く単語力を高めることができます。

「新・英単語センター1800」

君を熱誠指導でリードする

担任指導

志望校合格のために
君の力を最大限に引き出す

　定期的な面談を通じた「熱誠指導」で、最適な学習方法をアドバイス。スケジュールを具体的に示し、君のやる気を引き出します。課題をともに考え解決し、志望校合格までリードする存在、それが東進の「担任」です。

現役合格者の声

慶應義塾大学 文学部
根橋 里帆さん

　担任助手の先生には合格報告会での発表を聞いた時から憧れていました。毎週のグループ面談でアドバイスをいただき、「先生なしでは私の受験はうまくいかなかった」と言っても過言ではありません。

合格の秘訣3 東進ドットコム

ここでしか見られない受験と教育の情報が満載！
大学受験のポータルサイト

www.toshin.com

東進 検索
東進公式Twitter @Toshincom
東進公式Facebook www.facebook.com/ToshinHighSchool

東進ブックスのインターネット書店
東進WEB書店

ベストセラー参考書から
夢ふくらむ人生の参考書まで

学習参考書から語学・一般書までベストセラー＆ロングセラーの書籍情報がもりだくさん！あなたの「学び」をバックアップするインターネット書店です。検索機能もグンと充実。さらに、一部書籍では立ち読みも可能。探し求める1冊に、きっと出会えます。

スマホ・ケータイからもご覧いただけます

東進ドットコムはスマートフォン・ケータイから簡単アクセス！

最新の入試に対応!!
大学案内

偏差値でも検索できる。検索機能充実！

東進ドットコムの「大学案内」では最新の入試に対応した情報を様々な角度から検索できます。学生の声、入試問題分析、大学校歌など、他では見られない情報が満載！登録は無料です。
また、東進ブックスの『新大学受験案内』では、厳選した172大学を詳しく解説。大学案内とあわせて活用してください。

Web / Book

難易度ランキング　50音検索

172大学の過去問を無料で閲覧
大学入試過去問データベース

君が目指す大学の過去問をすばやく検索、じっくり研究!

東進ドットコムの「大学入試問題 過去問データベース」は、志望校の過去問をすばやく検索し、じっくり研究することが可能。172大学の過去問をダウンロードすることができます。センター試験の過去問も20年分以上掲載しています。登録は無料です。志望校対策の「最強の教材」である過去問をフル活用することができます。

学生特派員からの
先輩レポート

生の大学情報をリアルタイムに提供！

東進で頑張り難関大学に合格した先輩が、ブログ形式で大学の情報を提供します。大勢の学生特派員によって、大学案内・情報誌などにはない生の大学情報が次々とアップデートされていきます。また、受験を終えたからこそわかるアドバイスも、受験勉強に役立つこと間違いなしです。

付録 6

合格の秘訣4 東進模試

申込受付中
※お問い合わせ先は付録9ページをご覧ください。

学力を伸ばす模試

「自分の学力を知ること」が受験勉強の第一歩

■絶対評価の連続模試
毎回同じ判定基準で、志望校と現在の学力を比較。自分の成績の伸びが正確に把握できます。

■入試の『本番レベル』
「合格までにあと何点必要か」がわかる。早期に本番レベルを知ることができます。

■最短7日のスピード返却
成績表を、最短で実施7日後に返却。次の目標に向けた復習はバッチリです。

■合格指導解説授業
模試受験後に合格指導解説授業を実施。重要ポイントが手に取るようにわかります。

- 模試受験中に学力を伸ばす!
- 合格までの距離を知り、計画を立てる!
- 学習効果を確認、弱点を克服する!

全国統一高校生テスト
高3生 高2生 高1生 — 年1回

東進模試 ラインアップ 2014年度

模試名	対象	回数
センター試験本番レベル模試	受験生 高2生	年5回
センター試験高校生レベル模試	高2生 高1生	年4回
東大本番レベル模試	受験生	年3回
京大本番レベル模試	受験生	年3回
北大本番レベル模試	受験生	年2回
東北大本番レベル模試	受験生	年2回
名大本番レベル模試	受験生	年2回
阪大本番レベル模試	受験生	年2回
九大本番レベル模試	受験生	年2回
難関大本番レベル記述模試	受験生	年5回
有名大本番レベル記述模試	受験生	年5回
大学合格基礎力判定テスト	受験生 高2生 高1生	年4回
センター試験同日体験受験	高2生 高1生	年1回
東大入試同日体験受験	高2生	年1回

※センター試験本番レベル模試とのドッキング判定

※最終回がセンター試験後の受験となる模試は、センター試験自己採点とのドッキング判定となります。

東進で勉強したいが、近くに校舎がない君は…
東進ハイスクール 在宅受講コースへ

「遠くて東進の校舎に通えない……」。そんな君も大丈夫! 在宅受講コースなら自宅のパソコンを使って勉強できます。ご希望の方には、在宅受講コースのパンフレットをお送りいたします。お電話にてご連絡ください。学習・進路相談も随時可能です。

付録 7

2014年も難関大・有名大 ゾクゾク現役合格
現役合格実績 NO.1

現役のみ！講習生含まず！最終学年高3在籍者のみ！

※現役合格実績を公表している全国すべての塾・予備校の中で、表記の難関大合格実績実績において最大の合格者数です。
東進の合格実績には、高卒生や講習生、公開模試生を含みません。（他の大手予備校とは基準が異なります）

2014年3月31日締切

ついに達成!! 東大現役合格者の3人に1人が東進生

東進生現役占有率 33.6%

東大 現役合格者 668名（昨対+68名）

- 文Ⅰ…108名
- 理Ⅰ…227名
- 文Ⅱ…82名
- 理Ⅱ…113名
- 文Ⅲ…96名
- 理Ⅲ…42名

今年の東大合格者（前後期合計）は現浪あわせて3,109名。そのうち現役の合格者は1,988名。東進の現役合格者は668名ですので、東大現役合格者における東進生の占有率は33.6%となります。私たちが一つの大きな節目として目標に掲げてきた「3人に1人が東進生」をついに達成しました。合格者の皆さん、おめでとうございます！

現役合格 旧七帝大＋四大学連合 2,696名 昨対+249名

旧七帝大
- 東京大……668名
- 名古屋大……263名
- 京都大……246名
- 大阪大……380名
- 北海道大……220名
- 九州大……341名
- 東北大……181名

四大学連合
- 東京医科歯科大……38名
- 東京工業大……127名
- 一橋大……146名
- 東京外国語大……86名

現役合格 国公立医学部医学科 543名 昨対+22名

- 東京大(理科Ⅲ類)……42名
- 東京医科歯科大(医学部医学科)……19名
- 大阪市立大(医学部医学科)……8名
- 京都大(医学部医学科)……11名
- 横浜市立大(医学部医学科)……13名
- 神戸大(医学部医学科)……7名
- 北海道大(医学部医学科)……9名
- 新潟大(医学部医学科)……11名
- 岡山大(医学部医学科)……12名
- 東北大(医学部医学科)……9名
- 金沢大(医学部医学科)……7名
- 広島大(医学部医学科)……14名
- 名古屋大(医学部医学科)……9名
- 福井大(医学部医学科)……13名
- 山口大(医学部医学科)……14名
- 大阪大(医学部医学科)……14名
- 山梨大(医学部医学科)……13名
- 徳島大(医学部医学科)……13名
- 九州大(医学部医学科)……18名
- 信州大(医学部医学科)……7名
- 香川大(医学部医学科)……15名
- 旭川医科大(医学部医学科)……10名
- 岐阜大(医学部医学科)……12名
- 愛媛大(医学部医学科)……15名
- 弘前大(医学部医学科)……10名
- 浜松医科大(医学部医学科)……13名
- 高知大(医学部医学科)……7名
- 秋田大(医学部医学科)……7名
- 名古屋市立大(医学部医学科)……12名
- 佐賀大(医学部医学科)……20名
- 福島県立医科大(医学部)……8名
- 三重大(医学部医学科)……18名
- 長崎大(医学部医学科)……13名
- 筑波大(医学部医学科)……14名
- 滋賀医科大(医学部医学科)……8名
- 熊本大(医学部医学科)……9名
- 群馬大(医学部医学科)……13名
- 京都府立医科大(医学部医学科)……9名
- その他国公立大(医学部医学科)……54名
- 千葉大(医学部医学科)……12名

現役合格 早慶 4,210名 昨対+181名

- 早稲田大……2,757名
- 慶應義塾大……1,453名

東進生現役占有率 20.7%
4.9人に1人が東進生!!※

東進生現役占有率 23.2%
4.4人に1人が東進生!!※

上理明青立法中 昨対+1,408名
現役合格 13,498名

- 上智大……980名
- 東京理科大……1,621名
- 明治大……3,181名
- 青山学院大……1,382名
- 立教大……1,781名
- 法政大……2,656名
- 中央大……1,897名

関関同立 昨対+668名
現役合格 9,197名

- 関西学院大……1,589名
- 関西大……2,308名
- 同志社大……1,999名
- 立命館大……3,301名

私立医学部医学科 昨対+32名
現役合格 438名

☆防衛医科大学校を含む

現役合格 全国主要国公立大

北海道教育大	89名	横浜市立大	173名	奈良女子大	52名
弘前大	78名	新潟大	191名	和歌山大	62名
岩手大	45名	富山大	133名	鳥取大	94名
宮城大	30名	金沢大	180名	島根大	64名
秋田大	45名	福井大	59名	岡山大	212名
山形大	69名	山梨大	78名	広島大	268名
福島大	59名	信州大	157名	山口大	225名
筑波大	221名	岐阜大	124名	徳島大	113名
茨城大	145名	静岡大	182名	香川大	96名
宇都宮大	52名	静岡県立大	54名	愛媛大	177名
群馬大	70名	愛知教育大	94名	高知大	66名
埼玉大	147名	名古屋工業大	118名	北九州市立大	112名
埼玉県立大	37名	名古屋市立大	107名	佐賀大	105名
千葉大	382名	三重大	209名	長崎大	118名
首都大学東京	241名	滋賀大	95名	熊本大	177名
お茶の水女子大	58名	京都教育大	26名	大分大	63名
電気通信大	87名	大阪市立大	185名	宮崎大	59名
東京学芸大	119名	大阪府立大	175名	鹿児島大	92名
東京農工大	87名	大阪教育大	109名	琉球大	95名
横浜国立大	237名	神戸大	374名		

※東進調べ

ウェブサイトでもっと詳しく ➡ 東進 🔍検索

付録 **8**　各大学の合格実績は、東進ハイスクールと東進衛星予備校の合同実績です。

東進へのお問い合わせ・資料請求は
東進ドットコム www.toshin.com
もしくは下記のフリーダイヤルへ！

ハッキリ言って合格実績が自慢です！ 大学受験なら、
東進ハイスクール ☎ 0120-104-555 (トーシン ゴーゴーゴー)

●東京都
[中央地区]
市ヶ谷校	0120-104-205
新宿エルタワー校	0120-104-121
※新宿校大学受験本科	0120-104-020
高田馬場校	0120-104-770
人形町校	0120-104-075

[城北地区]
赤羽校	0120-104-293
本郷三丁目校	0120-104-068
茗荷谷校	0120-738-104

[城東地区]
綾瀬校	0120-104-762
金町校	0120-452-104
★北千住校	0120-693-104
錦糸町校	0120-104-249
豊洲校	0120-104-282
西新井校	0120-266-104
西葛西校	0120-289-104
門前仲町校	0120-104-016

[城西地区]
★池袋校	0120-104-062
大泉学園校	0120-104-862
荻窪校	0120-687-104
高円寺校	0120-104-627
石神井校	0120-104-159
巣鴨校	0120-104-780
成増校	0120-028-104
練馬校	0120-104-643

[城南地区]
大井町校	0120-575-104
蒲田校	0120-265-104
五反田校	0120-672-104
三軒茶屋校	0120-104-739
渋谷駅西口校	0120-389-104
下北沢校	0120-104-672
自由が丘校	0120-964-104
成城学園駅北口校	0120-104-616
千歳烏山校	0120-104-331
都立大学駅前校	0120-275-104

[東京都下]
★吉祥寺校	0120-104-775
国立校	0120-104-599
国分寺校	0120-622-104
立川駅北口校	0120-104-662
田無校	0120-104-272
調布校	0120-104-305
八王子校	0120-896-104
東久留米校	0120-565-104
府中校	0120-104-676
町田校	0120-104-507
武蔵小金井校	0120-480-104
武蔵境校	0120-104-769

●神奈川県
青葉台校	0120-104-947
厚木校	0120-104-716
川崎校	0120-226-104
湘南台東口校	0120-104-706
新百合ヶ丘校	0120-104-182
センター南駅前校	0120-104-722
たまプラーザ校	0120-104-445
鶴見校	0120-876-104
平塚校	0120-104-742
藤沢校	0120-104-549
向ヶ丘遊園校	0120-104-757
武蔵小杉校	0120-165-104
★横浜校	0120-104-473

●埼玉県
浦和校	0120-104-561
大宮校	0120-104-858
春日部校	0120-104-508
川口校	0120-917-104
川越校	0120-104-538
小手指校	0120-104-759
志木校	0120-104-202
せんげん台校	0120-104-388
草加校	0120-104-690
所沢校	0120-104-594
★南浦和校	0120-104-573
与野校	0120-104-755

●千葉県
我孫子校	0120-104-253
市川駅前校	0120-104-381
稲毛海岸校	0120-104-575
海浜幕張校	0120-104-926
★柏校	0120-104-353
北習志野校	0120-344-104
新浦安校	0120-556-104
新松戸校	0120-104-354
★千葉校	0120-104-564
★津田沼校	0120-104-724
土気校	0120-104-584
成田駅前校	0120-104-346
船橋校	0120-104-514
松戸校	0120-104-257
南柏校	0120-104-439
八千代台校	0120-104-863

●茨城県
つくば校	0120-403-104
土浦校	0120-059-104
取手校	0120-104-328

●静岡県
★静岡校	0120-104-585

●長野県
長野校	0120-104-586

●奈良県
JR奈良駅前校	0120-104-746
★奈良校	0120-104-597

★は高卒本科(高卒生)設置校
※は高卒生専用校舎

※変更の可能性があります。最新情報はウェブサイトで確認できます。

全国888校、10万人の高校生が通う、
東進衛星予備校 ☎ 0120-104-531 (トーシン ゴーサイン)

東進ドットコムでお近くの校舎を検索！

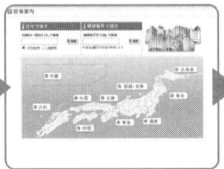

「東進衛星予備校」の「校舎案内」をクリック → エリア・都道府県を選択 → 校舎一覧が確認できます

資料請求もできます

近くに東進の校舎がない高校生のための
東進ハイスクール 在宅受講コース ☎ 0120-531-104 (ゴーサイン トーシン)

※2014年10月末現在